155

D1112493

THE HEBREW PROPHETIC CONSCIOUSNESS

THE
HEBREW PROPHETIC
CONSCIOUSNESS

by

HAROLD KNIGHT

M.A., B.Litt., D.Phil., B.D., (Oxon.)
Sometime Scholar of Oriel College, Oxford
Sixth Form Master at The King's School, Canterbury

LUTTERWORTH PRESS
LONDON and REDHILL

First published 1947

This book is produced in complete conformity with the authorized economy standards

Printed in Great Britain by
The Camelot Press Ltd., London and Southampton

CONTENTS

5

PROLEGOMENA

THE prophetic consciousness among the Hebrews represents a spiritual transformation of the two main types of prophecy current among primitive peoples —divinatory prophecy and ecstatic prophecy. It will be our contention that the former of these types of prophecy is native to the religious tradition of Israel, whilst the latter is an essentially alien element with which the Hebrews were brought into contact as a result of their settlement in the land of Canaan and their assimilation of Canaanite culture. In order to demonstrate this contention, as also in order to bring out the prophets' own view of their mentality, it will be necessary to take as our point of departure the basic assumptions of Hebrew anthropology and psychology. We shall therefore begin by a consideration of these.

The Hebrew approach to life is predominantly concrete, synthetic, and intuitive, for the Hebrew dwells upon that primitive plane of culture on which man's thinking is fashioned by his sensuous impressions. He is incapable of distinguishing between the physical and the metaphysical, the body and the mind. He is not interested in the precise delimitation of an idea, but in the rich personal experience of living contact with its concrete manifestation. Thought is not an independent activity existing in its own right: it is an integral part of action. Thought, together with the action in which it issues, intention, together with its result, form for him a complex which he experiences in its totality and is incapable of analysing. The word in Hebrew has not the mere mathematical value of an algebraic sign: there clings to it, like some subtle aroma, the suggestion of the primitive human sensation which it was originally created to denote.

The primitive concreteness of the Hebrew mentality is, above all, manifested with characteristic effect in the

Hebrew approach to the nature of man. For the Hebrew, man is not a being composed of two distinct and separable entities—body and soul—but an unanalysed complex psycho-physical unity. This follows from the *naïveté* of the Hebrew consciousness in which thought is subsumed beneath life, action and sense-impression. The Hebrew conception of the personality of man is that of an unbroken integrated unity which is identified with the animated body. It is highly significant that the Hebrew language has no special term either for body or soul, for Hebrew thought does not work in these categories which presuppose the metaphysical analysis of human life.

The Hebrew seeks to interpret the mystery of life by means of the two terms—*nephesh* (breath) and *ruach* (wind). The former is the breath-principle viewed as the centre and source of life in a human being (Gen. 35: 18; 1 Kings 17: 21; Job 2: 20, 31: 39, 33: 18; Ps. 16: 10, 30: 4, 31: 10, etc.). It is the bearer both of the animal life of physical appetite and desire, and of the higher psychical consciousness. It is referred back to the breath of Yahwe as its ultimate source but it is conceived as constituting the unique individuality of its human possessor. It is the fundamental soul-substance which is manifested in all that the individual person is and does.

Ruach, on the other hand, is an impersonal term which emphasizes man's absolute dependence upon God. Whereas it is usual to say my *nephesh*, in the sense of "I myself," it would be quite impossible to speak of my *ruach*. *Ruach*, properly denoting "wind", is thought of as the universal life-stream which flows from God and expresses the activity of God in the world which He has created. In its manifestations, *ruach* suggests the irresistible might of the wind which sweeps across vast desert spaces and in the track of which all things are driven helplessly hither and thither. In its essence it signifies mysterious, supernatural power which lies beyond man's control. It is the instrument of the effects wrought by Yahwe in the life of the world and of man, but it does not impart divinity, or bring about union with the divine. In the Hebrew consciousness, the immanent working of God seems to be specially connected with the elemental force of the wind. God walks or flies upon the wings of the wind (Ps. 18: 10, 104: 3); the winds are His messengers (Ps. 104: 4). The wind is the breath of God's mouth (Job 15: 30); by which the heavens were created (Ps. 33: 6); and the waters of the Red Sea piled up (Exod. 15: 8, 10). With the Hebrew incapacity to distinguish the physical from the psychical, this conception of the wind as a force emanating from God soon gave birth to the conception of the Spirit of God, which, operating as an invisible wind-like influence, produced supernormal effects in human life. The operation of the *ruach* came to be the accepted explanation of all that was striking or unusual in human conduct. It is applied to the wisdom of Joseph (Gen. 41: 38); to the skill of the craftsman (Exod. 31: 3); to the warrior-ideal of the Judges (Judges 3: 10); to the ecstatic frenzy of the prophet (Ezek. 2: 2).

In post-exilic days, *ruach* develops a new range of application which gives it an apparent approximation to *nephesh*. By the time of the Exile, it is probable that the wave of charismatic enthusiasm which swept over Syria had somewhat subsided, and the higher activities of the spirit are now acclimatized to the soil of humanity. *Ruach* is now so broadened in meaning that it appears almost as an alternative term for *nephesh*, since it can denote the breath of life in man (Ps. 146: 4; Ezek. 37: 9, 10; Gen. 6: 17; Job 9: 18, 15: 30, 19: 17); the interior moral and spiritual dispositions, especially anger, pride, etc. (Prov. 16: 18; Eccles. 7: 8; Ps. 78: 8), and the mental consciousness generally. This generalization of the term implies an increased emphasis upon the idea that man's life in all its reaches is under the sovereign control of God. Yahwe, like the Egyptian deity, breathes into both man and beast the breath (with all its psychical implicates) which makes them alive. Nevertheless, *ruach*, despite the new extension of its use, retains its own distinctive

9

associations. It expresses the fact that the deepest springs of life in man flow from the infinite and all-pervasive life of God which is poured out upon mankind from above. *Ruach* is conceived as something which enters into a man from outside. When he dies, God withdraws this vitalizing breath, but it could not be said that his *ruach* expires. *Nephesh*, on the other hand, is man's inalienable possession. It is his in virtue of the fact that he is a living being. Hence, it can be said that his *nephesh* dies. *Ruach* denotes the central zone of man's consciousness which is most readily accessible to the control of the invasive Spirit of God. But this subtle differentiation in the usage of the two terms in no way implies the break-up of the primitive Hebrew conception of man as a unity. The cardinal postulate of Hebrew psychology—that man is a physical organism animated by a breath-soul—remains unaffected.

It follows from this understanding of human nature that the Hebrew, unlike the Greek, recognizes no antithesis between flesh and soul. The true antithesis for the Hebrew is that between man and God, or between the human flesh-soul and the divine *ruach*. (Isa. 31: 3; Jer. 17: 5; Job 10: 4). So far from being contrasted, flesh and soul might almost be said to be fused, in Hebrew anthropology. The soul is a bundle of psychic energies, stamped with a certain character, and manifesting itself through the flesh. The life of the soul is indissolubly linked to that of the flesh; the idea of a discarnate soul is utterly foreign to the Hebrew mentality. The departed in Sheol are not souls freed from their bodies, but faint shadows of the former man, whose unified psycho-physical life is thus feebly prolonged. Yahwe's breathing into the clay does not mean that the dead body was animated by the infusion of a soul, but that it was changed into something living by becoming endowed with the life-giving breath.

This organic relation of body and soul results in the fact that, for the Hebrew, the spiritual consciousness of man is dispersed throughout the body and inheres in its various parts. The soul is identified with the various bodily organs through which it acts and manifests itself. Soul and body are fused with a completeness which it is difficult for us to understand. Physical sustenance reacts upon the soul, fortifying it: fasting afflicts the soul (Isa. 58: 3, 5; Num. 29: 7). The soul life pulsates throughout the body. Jeremiah's overflowing pity expresses itself in a roaring of the bowels (Jer. 31: 20). In the Psalms, the bones seem to register the whole gamut of the Psalmist's interior spiritual life (Ps. 35: 10, 51: 8, 6: 3, 31: 10). We may say that, in the consciousness of the Hebrew, the soul is felt to stamp ineffaceably every movement of the body.

The following study is put forward in the conviction that the Christian Church to-day, perhaps as much as in the decline of the Middle Ages, needs to be quickened and spiritualized by a fresh penetration to the depths of Biblical religious experience. By this is not meant simply a revival of "New Testament Christianity" as that phrase is generally understood in modern humanistic culture, but a new understanding of the creative religious faith which informs the Hebrew Bible. Apart from such an understanding, there can be no adequate appreciation of the Person and Work of Jesus Christ and of the religion which He founded. That great Semitic philologist and historian of religions—Ernest Renan—wrote in his *Souvenirs d'Enfance et de Jeunesse* with reference to his entry upon the final course of theological study at the Saint-Sulpice seminary: "La langue hébraïque était ici [in the interpretation of Holy Scripture] l'instrument capital, puisque, des deux Bibles chrétiennes, l'une est en hébreu et *que, même pour le Nouveau Testament, il n'y a pas de complète exégèse sans la connaissance de l'hébreu.*" In a world and in a Church, where, except in Germany, the current of theological thought has been decisively influenced during the modern era by the spirit of Greek and scientific rationalism, how little has the statement of Renan been understood and its implications realized!

In the study of the life of Christ, for example, how little has been understood the intimate mingling of Old and New Testaments, the fact that Jesus stands in complete solidarity with the spiritual nucleus of Israel, with the suffering poor and meek of the Psalms or the fact that His mind was saturated with Old Testament conceptions and constantly fed upon the deep sources of spirituality in the living religious traditions of His race! It is unfortunate that ecclesiastical and dogmatic theology, in particular, takes its rise from apostolic Christianity as petrified, rationalized, and hellenized by the impact of Greek culture. Thus the creative genius and its original interpretation of man and his destiny, *which are integrally connected with the religious consciousness of Israel*, are obscured.

It is also hoped that the present work may encourage and develop theological communion and sympathy between the Anglican and Free Churches. It is a pleasure to record the debt which I owe to my revered counsellor at Oxford, the late Principal Wheeler H. Robinson, the eminent Nonconformist divine who possessed so true and genuine an appreciation of the sacramental teaching of Catholic Christianity and its roots in the Semitic conception of life.

Finally, I have to thank the Editor of *Theology* for permission to re-print the chapter entitled "Divine Pathos", which appeared in a slightly modified form in the *Theology* of February, 1942.

HAROLD KNIGHT.

25 THE PRECINCTS,
CANTERBURY.
June, 1947.

SYNOPSIS OF CONTENTS

PART ONE: HISTORY AND PSYCHOLOGY

CHAPTER I

The Historical Genesis of the Hebrew Prophetic Consciousness

The Hebrew prophetic consciousness is a complex product which may be traced back to the two types of prophecy recognized in the ancient world—divinatory prophecy and ecstatic prophecy. It is the former of these two ways of prophecy which is native to the religious tradition of Israel. The latter is an essentially alien element with which the Hebrews came into contact after their settlement in the land of Canaan. The truth of this contention is shown by the consideration that there is a fundamental disparity between the religious psychology underlying ecstatic phenomena and the theology and psychology which govern the prophetic religion of the Old Testament. Ecstatic experience leads straight to the conclusion that man is an incarnate soul which is inherently divine, whereas Hebrew psychology presupposes that man is an animated body and that his spiritual consciousness is diffused through its physical organs. Our thesis is confirmed by an examination of the characteristic activities of the more considerable prophetic figures who preceded the writing prophets. Samuel, like the heathen soothsayer Balaam, is a seer and the typical form of his experience is, not ecstasy, but the night-vision. Elijah is a rainmaker who stands out in sharpest contrast to the professional ecstatic of his day. In the figure of Elisha we see the primitive tradition of magic and divination becoming associated with ecstatic prophecy and preparing us for the complex structure of the Hebrew prophetic consciousness.

As regards the writing prophets themselves, it is their understanding of the word, and the symbolic action, which proves that their consciousness can be traced back to its primitive roots in Semitic divination and magic. Nevertheless, an impassable gulf separates the Hebrew prophet from the Semitic diviner. The diviner acts on his own personal initiative; the prophet, in response to the initiative of God. The prophets' religious transformation of divination is reached, historically, through vitalizing contact with Canaanite ecstasy.

CHAPTER 2

Prophetic Vision and Ecstasy in the Light of Hebrew Psychology

The prophets of Israel borrow the forms of manticism current in their religious environment, but lend to them a new spiritual significance by informing them with the spirit of their own religious psychology. The ecstatic vision becomes a medium through which is expressed the prophets' inspired insight into the inner spiritual realities determining imminent events. The ecstatic sense of compulsion is not the god-intoxication of heathen ecstasy but the invasive transforming energy of the Spirit of God through the impact of which the prophets' personality is quickened to a new intensity of consciousness. The unified psycho-physical personality is not impaired or dissolved, but transfigured. The physical organs, conceived as the seat of spiritual consciousness, are subjected to divine control. Inspiration is mediated through the divine use of the prophets' sense impressions. The prophet detaches that part of himself, viz., the mouth, which is understood to be specially subjected to the sway of the divine and expresses his conviction of the validity of his message by declaring that his words are the words of Yahwe.

CHAPTER 3

The Writing Prophets and the Nebiim

The writing prophets are locked in violent conflict with the official *nebiim* of their day, but are compelled to designate their own inspired activity as prophesying. Jepsen solves the problem which thus emerges by denying all connexion between the writing prophet and the *nabi*, declaring that the former repudiates the spirit-possession which is the distinctive feature in the experience of the latter. The problem does not admit of so facile a solution. The distinction between the writing prophets and their predecessors cannot be grounded in psychological considerations at all. The writing prophets do not attack spirit-possession, as such, but inveigh against its artificial simulation by a class of persons who have ceased to experience the living power of the Spirit. The difference between the writing prophets and their predecessors is that between higher and lower levels of spiritual consciousness. In the case of the charismatic *nabi*, attention is focused on the unusual psychological form which his experience takes; but, with the writing prophet, the psychological accompaniments are incidental rather than essential. The writing prophet is the fine flower of the *nabi* movement. The conflict between the canonical prophets and the official *nebiim* of their day can only be understood on the hypothesis that in Judah the *nebiim* evince a gradual approximation to the priest-prophets of the Canaanite sanctuaries. As Jeremiah came gradually to realize, the ultimate test of the genuineness of inspiration is to be sought, not in the technical forms which mediate it, but in the reality of the religious communion which underlies it and the spiritual fruits it produces. The deep distinction between the Biblical prophet and the false prophet consists in the fact that, whereas the authority of the former is spiritual, inward and intrinsic, the authority of the latter is formal, official and extrinsic. This antithesis generates a clash between their respective theologies. The theology of the former is living, anchored in the creative movement of personal spiritual life: the theology of the latter is rationalized and nationalistic, conditioned by professional ties.

CHAPTER 4

The Religious Psychology of the Hebrew Prophetic Consciousness

In a discussion of the psychology of the prophetic consciousness, it is of the utmost importance to define the precise shade of meaning we are to attach to the term ecstasy. Critics, e.g., Hölscher, have usually taken this term to connote a psychopathic state. Such an understanding of the term is relevant only to the peripheral elements of the prophetic consciousness and does not enable us to penetrate the psychology of its central zone. In its wider and deeper meaning, ecstasy denotes an enhanced and quickened consciousness characterized by a vivid sense of knowing. It is in this connotation that the term may be most usefully applied to the interpretation of the prophetic consciousness. The inspired state of mind which compels the utterance "*Ko amar Yahwe*" is one in which there takes place such a simplification and unification of the prophet's being as gives rise to a deep emotional realization of truth. This state of mind is one of experimental communion with God. But there is a vital distinction between prophet and mystic; for whereas, with the mystic, the incommunicable experience is an end in itself, with the prophet, the inspired consciousness is but a means by which he receives a divine message for his fellow men. The prophets show themselves to be eminently rational, lucid and sane, but reason is not the source of their oracles. Their prophesying springs from an intuitive apprehension of truth, which results in a quickening of all their faculties of mind. The theological truths which may be elicited from their prophecies are logical implicates of that fundamental prophetic experience wherein the soul is confronted by the living God.

15

PART TWO: THEOLOGY

CHAPTER I

Revelation and Authority

Revelation is not the quasi-magical impartation of abstract truth but such an apprehension of living truth as is integral to the soul's dynamic experience of fellowship with God. God is the subject, not the object, of revelation; and the revelation, though objective, is intimately fused with the prophets' personality. In the moment of revelation there is an ultimate synthesis resulting from the inconceivable closeness of God with man. The prophets' revealed knowledge of God is continuous with and represents the culmination of other forms of intuitive knowledge—sense-perception, the awareness of beauty, and the knowledge of other selves. In all such knowledge the mind of the knower is at once active and passive. He is passive in so far as he is supremely receptive of a transcendent reality which impinges upon his consciousness from without; he is active in that an intensely awakened consciousness is required for the adequate recognition of the reality which is thus intruded upon his notice. The God with whom the prophets have to do is an inescapable Presence whose self-revelation is mediated to them through other forms of awareness, e.g., sense-perception, which, in Hebrew prophecy, is a creative source of spiritual suggestion.

The authority to which the prophets may lay claim is the authority which emanates from their unique capacity to receive revelation—their supreme awareness of Ultimate Reality. That this is a kind of knowledge which is not rationally discoverable is not a valid objection against it, since the simplest sense perception is equally irrational and mysterious. The speculative reason cannot be admitted as a final test of the validity of revelation, since the revelational knowledge of the prophet is akin to the vision of the poet and artist, and, under the abstracting operation of intellectual analysis, the character of reality as experienced simply evaporates. Revelation must vindicate itself at the bar of man's conscience and spiritual judgment, and in so far as man recognizes its spiritual intrinsic authority, he surrenders himself to the Spirit of God active within him.

CHAPTER 2

The Nature of Man and its Relation to God

The spiritual receptiveness of the prophet argues some kind of kinship between man and God. The mode and the significance of the prophetic experience (resting upon Hebrew psychology and theology) forbid us to conceive this kinship on the lines of pantheistic mysticism which postulates the inherent divinity of the soul. The doctrine of divine immanence which the prophetic consciousness implies is that man's life is mysteriously comprehended and determined in the eternal life of God. Human nature is not a finished product some element of which might constitute a special link with its divine Author. It is being continuously fashioned by God to be the vehicle of the divine Word. The humanity of man is realized in the process of the soul's dramatic fellowship with God.

CHAPTER 3

The Personality of God

The idea of the personality of God is central to the theology implied in the prophetic consciousness. It determines all the other theological implicates such as the divine passibility and the activity of the Eternal in the time series.

The prophets' call to prophesy may be viewed as the pressure exercised by absolute moral values upon their spirits. The characteristics of this religious experience show that the values apprehended therein are ultimate and objective. The nature of value is such that it has no meaning apart from personal life, and therefore the values which dominate the consciousness of the prophets must have their ground in the eternal, personal, God.

A second line of argument for personality in God derives also from the peculiar characteristics of the prophets' religious experience. This experience is essentially one of fellowship between persons, and, as such, is sharply contrasted with a certain type of mystical consciousness wherein the finite self is dissolved in the all-embracing unity of the Absolute. For the extreme mystic, personality constitutes a limiting condition to be overcome; whereas, for the prophet, it is the very basis of religious life. These contrasted attitudes reflect the paradox inherent in the very notion of personality, which, viewed from one angle, consists in the consciousness of the distinctness of the personal self, and viewed from another angle, arises through the transcendence of that self.

If, with the mystic, we consider God as the Absolute, it is difficult to predicate of Him personality which involves relationship and purposive activity. But the conditions for the growth of personality in human life need not attach to the idea itself. Personality is the highest principle of unity that we know, and thus the idea of a personal God affords the only secure basis for the unity of existence. Only a personal God can be understood both to transcend the world and to include it at the heart of His own eternal life.

CHAPTER 4

Divine Pathos

God is revealed to the prophets, not in the hidden changeless simplicity of His eternal being, but in the specific and pathetic determination of that being by the world of man. One aspect of the prophetic consciousness consists in the prophets' solidarity with the divine pathos. The passibility of God which is thus implied conflicts with the affirmations of traditional and classical Christian theology which is rooted in the Greek conception of divinity as changeless. Such *a priori* notions of deity proceed from the spirit of theological rationalism, but the prophetic consciousness opens up the dimension of eternal living Personality which defies interpretation in terms of the categories furnished by reason alone. The feeling-consciousness which the prophets ascribe to God may not be adequately conceived on the analogy of feeling in man (which is often a mark of servitude) but points to a conception of God as personal holy Will. Divine pathos makes possible a dynamic relationship between man and God, and a vital inter-relation between time and eternity. It implies that the righteousness of God is the inmost quality of His personal being, and that the moral government of the world is subjective. God reacts personally to man's sin, by the way of sacrificial suffering. The suffering in God which is thus suggested does not signify unhappiness and frustration, but the very means of divine victory and a constitutive element in the divine joy and blessedness.

CHAPTER 5

Time and Eternity

The fundamental character of prophetic revelation raises the problem of the relation between time and eternity. The prophetic awareness of God is the awareness of the divine demand mediated through some time-situation, a right reaction to which is the means whereby man realizes his fellowship with God. The eternal truth which the prophet apprehends is seen as inextricably involved in some temporal setting. This accords with the general viewpoint of the Hebrew who has no metaphysical understanding of time and eternity, but instinctively grasps the invincible finality of the time series, and feels eternity to be expressed within it. Time is not a closed circle, cut off from the ultimate source of being: its significance is derived from the fact that it expresses a spiritual drama which takes place in eternity. By implication, the Hebrew prophet contradicts the formal and rationalist conception of eternity as a *Nunc Stans* in which temporal successiveness vanishes. He implies that time has ontological reality because it is taken up into the heart of eternity itself.

CHAPTER 6

History

The view of time and eternity as vitally interrelated is one which gives birth to the conception of history. Whereas the historian interprets events in terms of their immediate psychological, biological, or economic causation, the Hebrew prophet interprets them in terms of their ultimate determination in eternity. The prophets are the exponents of the inner spiritual destiny of Israel which springs from the dramatic interaction of man and God on the plane of history. The historical event becomes revelatory of the divine because it is subjected to the overruling omnipotence of God and made to subserve the ends He has chosen. Thus arises the doctrine of Divine Providence. History contains at its heart an inner spiritual principle which enables it to transcend itself. The prophet's distinctive gift is that of foretelling, because he possesses the key to the interior spiritual dynamism of history.

PART ONE

HISTORY AND PSYCHOLOGY

Chapter One

THE HISTORICAL GENESIS OF THE HEBREW PROPHETIC CONSCIOUSNESS

A STUDY of the Hebrew prophetic consciousness should revolve around the term which is normally used in Hebrew, to designate the prophet, viz., *nabi*. Other terms there are which denote seer and diviner, e.g., *roeh* (ראה), *chozeh* (חזה), *qosem* (קסם); but *nabi* is the term which established itself as the official designation of the recognized prophet. It appears that this term was introduced into the language under the influence of the Canaanite culture which the Hebrews so rapidly absorbed, and that it was employed to refer to one who exercised an activity specially connected with the Canaanite sanctuaries.[1] The term thus came to designate a person who was peculiarly susceptible to ecstatic excitement, and its verbal form, whether used in the *Niphal* or the *Hithpael*, generally means, in the first stage of its development, to be in a raving condition. Yet, even from the first, a second idea was associated with this root, viz., that of announcing a message of which the frenzied *nabi* is the unconscious medium. When the fit of ecstasy is upon him, the *nabi* becomes the mouthpiece of the gods who convey through him a message to others. Thus, it was expected that the ecstasy of the Baal prophets on Mount Carmel would be attested by a divine communication from the unseen world. Now the Biblical history of the term shows a marked tendency for the former signification (rave) to be ousted by the latter (announce a divine message). Jepsen[2] has shown that whereas about 800 B.C. both the *Niphal* and *Hithpael* forms were used almost exclusively in the sense of "rave", by the latter half of the sixth century, the

[1] See art. *in Ency. Brit.* by Harnack and McGiffert, p. 442; also Kautzsch, *Hast. Dict. Bible*, Extra Vol., p. 653

[2] *Nabi*, p. 8

meaning "deliver the Word of God" alone survives. This linguistic evolution faithfully mirrors the religious development of Old Testament prophecy. In its earliest stages it was practically indistinguishable from the sacred madness of the prophets who were attached to the Canaanite sanctuaries; yet, even so, it was recognized, in Canaan as well as in Israel, that the essence of prophecy lay in the inspired communication of the will of the gods concerning some concrete situation in human life. From the first, the *nabi* was clearly to be differentiated from the mystic, although the form of his special prophetic experience bears the most striking resemblance to mystical states of union with the divine. The transition from the earlier to the later usage reflects a gradual shifting of the centre of gravity. The emphasis which at first lay upon the unusual and arresting features of the prophet's state of mind, upon the psychology of his experience, is later transferred to the inner significance of that experience, and to the spiritual vision which it mediated.

In the early references to the prophetic consciousness which we find in the First Book of Samuel, it is the enthusiastic character of the prophetic bands which is vividly depicted and presented to us. The element of revelation is lost sight of in the wonder and awe which the eccentric conduct of these gregarious *nebiim* evidently arouses in their contemporaries. The prophetic ecstasy arises in closest connexion with the cult, and is stimulated by the liturgical music and dancing which from time immemorial accompanied it. It manifested itself in violent bodily motions, in confused and unintelligible utterances, and in insensibility to pain. It fed upon the haunting terror and the magic of darkness. We may imagine the prophets whirling themselves around the altar at the time of the sacrifice, brandishing and cutting themselves with swords and knives. In the earliest times, they doubtless believed that, by the due performance of the motions proper to the sacred dance, they were exercising a constraining influence over the god and compelling him to draw near to his worshippers. The feelings are raised to the highest degree of tension, the world seems transfigured, the personality of the prophet undergoes a subtle change. Sundered from the existence of every day, rapt beyond its dissatisfactions, he becomes subject to hallucination, and shares in the life of the gods themselves. Pain is no longer felt as pain, but only serves to intensify the ecstasy. The soul is now freed from its bodily shackles, and soars upward until it is able to see and hear things beyond mortal ken. Such were the prophets whom Saul met at Mount Gibeah, and with whose enthusiasm he himself became so easily infected (1 Sam. 10: 5 ff., 19: 18 ff.).

Was this ecstasy an exotic phenomenon in Israel, and is it the sole root from which the Hebrew prophetic consciousness springs? It has been maintained that ecstatic prophecy was not a native product of the religion of Israel, that it is an element of that Canaanite culture which so profoundly modified Israel's religious outlook.[1] This view seems to be substantially correct. So far as our records go, it would appear that only from the days of the early monarchy onwards does the activity of ecstatic prophets become a noticeable feature of the national religion. About this time the *nebiim* begin to secure their niche in the sociological structure: they assume the importance of a class, conscious of its dignity and worth. They claim the right, like Samuel, to anoint and depose kings, to rebuke those in authority and to determine the direction of national policy. They are the inheritors of the charismatic leadership of the Judges. In southern Israel, they ally themselves with the priesthood and attain an authoritative position at the royal court.[2] In northern Israel, though despised for their social inferiority, and failing to obtain the favour of monarchy and priesthood, they can nevertheless instil terror by the wonder-working, quasi-magical powers which are at their command: their persons and their possessions, their words and their deeds are imbued with that numinous

[1] Hölscher, *Die Profeten*, p. 140   [2] Jepsen, *op. cit.*, p. 154

mana which is fraught with such terrible dangers for primitive man.[1] In the spectacular development of ecstatic prophesying, the religion of Israel appears to be taking a new departure. The records yield no reliable evidence of a similar movement having taken place at an earlier period. It is true that the word *nabi* is applied to various leading figures of the national past, e.g., to Moses and Abraham,[2] but it is quite certain that here we have to do with a revision carried out under the influence of the later prophetic movement. Nor is there any evidence that ecstatic prophecy was ever a clearly-marked feature of Semitic religion in general. Ecstasy is a type of religion which cannot have been specially congenial to the Semites, who were distinguished by their sober, practical judgment, and their acute observation of the world. They shared with all primitive peoples the reigning idea of demonic possession, and ascribed the divination of their prophets to possession by an indwelling *sahib*, but manticism of this kind may not be equated with ecstatic fervour. The mantic ecstasy of Balaam belongs to quite a different genre from that of the infectious spiritual enthusiasm of the prophets of Baal or the worshippers of Dionysos. Whereas the experience of the latter rests upon the presupposition that the soul of man is divine and can be freed from its imprisonment in the body by means of the sacred cultic dance, the experience of Balaam is much nearer to that of the Arabian *kahin* who is compelled to utter in rhythmic speech the whispered suggestions of his mysterious demonic companion—his *sahib*. Here we are confronted by two radically different types of inspired prophecy— each belonging to its own peculiar *Weltanschauung*. The one arises in a relatively cultivated world, with its settled priesthood, its time-honoured sanctuaries, its quite advanced conception of the spiritual psyche. The other is proper to the religion of desert nomads who needed no priest or sanctuary, who had not the spiritual enlightenment to conceive of the soul as an *anima*, and whose main

---

[1] Jepsen, pp. 163 ff.   [2] Gen. 20: 7; Deut. 34: 10; Hos. 12: 14

concern was to destroy their enemies by the help of a divination not far removed from primitive magic.

It seems, then, that it is a mistake to seek the antecedents of Hebrew ecstatic prophesying in the earlier nomadic stage of their religion. All that we can find suggestive of the later development are such elements of the cultic ecstasy as are common to primitive religions generally.

In order to prove that ecstatic phenomena are alien to the religion of Israel, it suffices to draw out the deeper characteristics and presuppositions of this type of religious experience.

The psychological factors that determine ecstasy are clear. It is a type of religion that arises out of the soul's need to overcome the limitations involved in its separate existence, to escape from the insipidity of the everyday world and to merge itself for a brief space in the all-embracing One whose divine life, imparted to each individual soul, is obscured and cramped by the fetters of the flesh. The violent stimulation of feeling and senses, characteristic of ecstasy, has as its object the suspension of the normal consciousness and the consequent release of the soul into union with its divine source. By the use of means such as music, dancing, narcotics, etc., the practitioner of ecstasy aims at producing an enlargement of his being which will enable him to transcend the barriers of his private self and to become lost in the realm of the supra-personal and the divine.

Now, religion of this kind presupposes certain definite, if half-conscious, beliefs about God and the soul which at every point contradict the characteristic Hebrew approach to God and man. *In Hebrew religion, it is the fear of the numinous which is the predominant factor.* Man, stamped with the frailty of the flesh, feels that he is separated from God by an infinite distance which his own personal exertions cannot overcome. The ecstatic, on the contrary, feels that his soul is surrounded by the divine and that, by assiduous training and ascetic discipline, it can become merged in the mighty flood of the divine life. Ecstasy is the outcome of the *attraction* which the divine exercises over the life of the soul. It is the fruit of subjective longing and aspiration. So far from being prostrated in trembling awe, the soul grasps boldly the object of its passionate love, until in the ardour of the embrace it becomes one with the beloved. The ultimate term of ecstatic experience is union and absorption—the dissolution of personality in the all-pervasive Divine. The final expression of the Hebrew religious consciousness is the prophetic fellowship with God. Communion, involving a fellowship of persons, as opposed to union, involving the dissolution of distinctions, is the only appropriate term to apply to the religion of the prophets. The personality of the prophet stands out all the more sharply in the stress of his dramatic dialogue with God.

Ecstasy is an incommunicable experience which is deliberately cultivated as an end in itself. It is remote from the historical and concrete. It involves a world-renouncing attitude, as well as a loss of self-conscious personality. It is brought about by systematic preparation. Prophetic religion is diametrically opposed to all these characteristics. The prophet is never conscious of his religious experience as an end to be aimed at. It is determined wholly by the initiative of God, from whose overpowering approach he recoils in fear and self-abasement. The prophet is world-affirming, engaged in the bitter *Sturm und Drang* of contemporary life. His object is not to attain the ineffable bliss of anonymous ecstasy, but to report divine judgment on the historical and the concrete. His experience is determined by a divine commission which he has done nothing to merit and which is thrust upon him from the outside.

Again, the god of the ecstatic is not conceived anthropomorphically but as a spirit analogous to the soul substance in man. The divine is considered as fluid, supra-personal, all-pervasive: at any moment it may invade and supersede the soul of a human being, giving messages through his vocal organs and imprinting upon him a sacred character. In this circle of ideas we have a

spiritual conception of divinity which forms a strong contrast to the anthropomorphic religion of the Hebrews.
The Bible presents us with theophanies—unsought manifestations of Yahwe in human tangible form, fraught with
terrible danger to mortal man. The presupposition of
such stories is that man cannot behold God and live.
Such a narrative as that of Manoah and his wife (Judges
13: 22) points to a religious environment in which man
lived in fear of the dangerous possibility of becoming
exposed to these intrusions of the divine. Ecstasy lies at
the furthest remove from such ideas. Instead of God
descending to the earth in the crushing glory of His
majesty, man cultivating ecstasy endeavours to raise
himself to the sphere of divinity. Instead of an infinite
distance separating God from the worshipper and overwhelming the latter, man in ecstasy comes so near to
God that the dividing line between humanity and
divinity is obliterated.

Another proof that ecstatic prophesying was not
native to Israel rests upon psychological and anthropo-
logical considerations. Ecstasy implies the notion of the
spiritual psyche. It is an attempt to liberate the god within
the breast. It presupposes that man's nature is composed
of two separable entities, so distinct as to become almost
antagonistic to each other—the material prison-house of
the flesh, and the spiritual soul incarnate within it. This
incarnate soul was inherently divine, akin to the surrounding spirit-world towards which it aspired with
passionate longing, and where was its true home and
origin. Of course, the ecstatic did not always realize the
psychology implied in his religious experience, and the
belief in the divinity of the soul was developed by
reflection upon the nature of that experience. For, in the
ecstatic state, it seemed that the soul was transported
utterly outside the bounds of bodily existence; that it
became conscious of a divinity residing within itself and
of its own unlimited capacity to enjoy divine life.

An impassable gulf separates these beliefs from the
Hebrew understanding of man. We have seen that the

Hebrews were precluded by the very nature of their mentality from entertaining any distinct notion of the soul as an independent spiritual entity. Neither *nephesh* nor *ruach* can be taken simply as denoting the soul, for, though these terms are predominantly used to designate the spiritual consciousness of man, this consciousness is never abstracted from the integrated psycho-physical unity of man's being. The only idea of the soul which the Hebrews possessed was an inheritance from primitive culture. We refer to the conception of the *physical* psyche. This in the outlook of primitive people was understood to be a faint vaporous essence, a shadowy replica of the visible man which became active only in dreams and swoons. That the Hebrews were familiar with the notion of the *physical* psyche is proved by the character of their belief in Sheol.

By a number of important factors, then, the prophetic religious experience is decisively separated from the characteristics which distinguish mystical ecstasy in all times and places. A brief summary of these factors will perhaps contribute to the elucidation of our argument.

The occurence of ecstatic phenonema in the experience of the Hebrew prophets is abnormal, adventitious, spontaneous. Ecstasy, for them, is an outward, accidental, psychological, form: it indicates the peculiar psychic state which their inspiration in certain circumstances tended to assume. It is never the guarantee or the medium of religious communion. It is never to be regarded as the norm to which the psychology of the religious consciousness should approximate. It is, therefore, not an ideal to be striven after or a state to be deliberately induced. Never is it suggested that such moments of ecstatic vision are the culminating point of the religious life, or a primary means to the attainment of the knowledge of God. It would be a serious mistake to suppose that the I-formula—denoting the placing of God's word in the prophet's mouth—is to be interpreted with reference to the type of consciousness generally described by the phrase *unio mystica*. Such a type of con-

sciousness reposes upon certain metaphysical presuppositions which are wholly alien to the Hebrew world-view.
The chief of these presuppositions is the belief in the
Seelengrund—the belief that man's being is in itself a
medium of divine self-revelation; that man contains
within the depths of his soul an organ for the attainment
of communion with and knowledge of the divine.
Ecstatic mysticism proceeds from an intense cultivation
of the interior life as a result of which man sees the divine
emerge within the hidden, silent depths of personal
being. Now, in Hebrew anthropology man is never
endowed with this degree of independent dignity over
against the might and majesty of his Creator. Man has
no "soul" by the training of which he can climb the
ladder leading to the ecstatic vision of God. The substance of his entire being is stamped with the characteristic frailty of *basar* (flesh); *ruach* (spirit) is the essential
quality of the divine, its permanent indwelling in man
is a development of post-exilic theology. Man is utterly
devoid of any faculty by means of which he might attain
to the inner seeing of God in the hiddenness of the
interior life. Thus, he can never be the initiator of the
process by which he reaches knowledge of things divine.
The initiator must ever be God; not man. In accordance
with this fundamental necessity, the religion shaped by
the Jewish prophets is the religion of God's self-revelation
to man through the sacramental media of concrete event
and circumstance; not a religion of mystical aspiration
and communion. The characteristic religious attitude of
the prophets is not that of introspective brooding, issuing
in inner spiritual enlightenment; it is rather subordina-
tion and obedience to the divine Word which comes to
them from without and is invested with the palpable
authority of a divine command.

Further, the religion of the prophets, though in one
sense it is based upon the testimony of personal experience, is yet not individualistic; it is hardly to be thought
of in isolation from the corporate religious life of the
nation. It is true that the prophet is usually contrasted

with the people, as the God-inspired leader who is battling fiercely against the stubborn perversity of his contemporaries. But the message addressed to the prophet is concerned almost wholly with the destiny of the people, and the prophet himself is addressed primarily as Israel's representative before God. The subject of prophetic religion is not the individual soul of the prophet, but the people of Yahwe. The special character of the prophetic religious experience is a natural development from the unique covenant relationship which is the basis and the distinguishing mark of Israel's religion as a whole.

Again, the content of the prophetic experience, in contra-distinction to mystical-ecstatic states, is not primarily a peculiarly vivid and enhanced emotional consciousness of the divine presence. It is not incommunicable, *gefühlsmässig*, private; it is a rational, intelligible, essentially communicable divine Word directed to certain particular circumstances of the national life.

Moreover, it is to be noted that throughout the history of the prophetic movement there is a significant difference between mere psychic phenomena such as violent manifestations of ecstatic possession, and the essential characteristics of the great prophets, of their office and function in the national life. The former is an ever-recurrent and universal feature of the psychological forms of man's religious experience. The point to be emphasized about such an experience, however, is its explosive, spasmodic, temporary character. It is no abiding possession, it does not necessarily initiate a man into deeper spiritual communion with God, nor does it, in the case of the earlier gregarious *nebiim*, issue in the inspired announcement of new truth, or the declaration of the divine meaning inherent in some historical situation. The primary factor in the religious consciousness of the great prophets, however, from Moses to Deutero-Isaiah, is their experience of the Word, the call to the fulfilment of a momentous mission, and the initiation into a deeper and closer fellowship with God

than was common among their fellows. This contrast is
first indicated by the editors of the Book of Numbers in
the distinction which they draw between the spiritual
status of Moses and the seventy Elders on whom the
Spirit descended. Moses' nearness to God is such that
his communion with the divine appears direct and
immediate. "The Lord spake unto Moses face to face as
a man speaketh unto his friend" (Exod. 33: 11). In the
accounts which we have of his dramatic and dynamic
intercourse with God there is no suggestion of any
mantic form—spirit-possession, dream or vision—
through which revelation is mediated. Whereas divine
communications are made to official prophets by means
of dream and vision which require interpretation, that
is, through a recognized sacramental channel, to Moses
is granted the high privilege that God speaks to him
direct—mouth to mouth, even manifestly and not in
dark speeches (Num. 12: 8).

He is thus initiated into an esoteric communion with
God, which lies outside the normal and covenanted
mode of God's self-revelation to prophets. The Spirit of
God rests upon him, not in the sense of any violent
temporary disturbance such as ecstatic spirit-possession,
but as part and parcel of his very being.

In contrast to this calm and permanent spirituality of
Moses, the manifestation of the Spirit in the seventy
Elders is explosive, transient, confined to one single
occasion: they prophesied, we are told, but they did so
no more (Num. 11: 25). Whatever this prophesying was
it is certain that it cannot have been the declaration of
some Word of God, illuminating the ultimate significance
of a time-situation. We have here rather, an outpouring
of the Spirit, producing temporarily eccentric behaviour,
and regarded as qualifying the Elders for co-operation
with Moses in his work of leadership.

Hebrew psychology, with its stress upon the animated
body as the organ of personality, is obviously unfavourable to the development of an ecstatic type of religion.
The Hebrew religious consciousness, possessing the

characteristics to which we have referred, cannot have
been the matrix from which ecstatic prophesying emerged.
We may therefore accept the hypothesis that the ecstatic movement emanated from the religious environment with which the Israelites were brought into contact
after their settlement in the land of Canaan.

Seeing that ecstatic prophesying represents a type of
religion which cannot have been congenial and native to
Israel, the question arises whether the consciousness of
the great prophets reposes solely upon this foundation,
or whether it may be regarded as a development from
more remote origins. Jepsen puts forward the challenging
hypothesis that no other type of prophecy is discoverable
in the religious origins of Israel, and that ecstatic prophecy arose to supply a need experienced by those for
whom the priestly oracle was not within easy reach.[1]
According to this view, the various terms applied in the
Old Testament with reference to the prophetic class—
roeh, chozeh, nabi, qosem—reflect the various modes in
which God reveals Himself to the charismatic *nabi*. However much it may be possible on the basis of these
references to define and distinguish differing types of
prophetic consciousness, these types do not correspond
to different historical groups, reaching back to the
nomadic stage of the nation's development. The important archæological note which we find in the Old
Testament itself (1 Sam. 9: 9), to the effect that "he
that is now called a prophet was beforetime called a
seer", is discounted on the grounds that it means no
more than a variation of terminology; that the name
roeh originally used to denote a specialized form of the
prophetic consciousness of the *nabi* gradually dropped
out of use.[2] The term *nabi* is employed to denote a
member of that class of men to whom is imparted a
direct, inspired knowledge of the Will of God; and
Samuel is the first Israelite prophet of whom we have
any authentic record.[3] The characteristic sign, the
authentication of the *nabi*, consists simply in his posses-

[1] *op. cit.*, p. 149   [2] *op. cit.*, p. 54   [3] *op. cit.*, p. 151

sion of the Spirit; and even those forms of prophetic activity—wonder-working, healing miracles and the like —which seem to point back to the primitive past of the magician and medicine-man, are deprived by Jepsen of this historical significance and interpreted as diverse manifestations of the Spirit's power. Thus Jepsen, confining himself to a minute examination, though somewhat drastic handling, of the text, and setting aside the methods proper to *Religionsgeschichte*, comes to the interesting conclusion that all references to prophecy in the Old Testament have to do with the charismatic *Nabitum* itself—like the standing army and bureaucratic government, a product of an age of transition when the old nomadic traditions and social frame-work were rapidly disintegrating under the powerful impact of an alien and more advanced kind of culture.[1] The assimilation of Canaanite *Nabitum* was part of this process of adaptation to a new sociological setting. *Nabitum* is envisaged by Jepsen predominantly in its social aspect rather than as a variety of the religious consciousness.

In opposition to Jepsen, we would maintain that Hebrew prophecy, flowering in the eighth century, has its roots in a continuous religious tradition going back to a remote past, and that, though this tradition is decisively re-orientated by its contact with the ecstatic movement of Syria, it remains to the end as one of the prime determining factors in the growth of the Hebrew prophetic consciousness. The tradition to which we refer can be traced back historically to primitive Semitic magic and divination. The reason for adopting this hypothesis is that a careful examination of the character and activities of the leading prophetic figures prior to the eighth century—Balaam, Samuel, Elijah and Elisha— leads irresistibly to the conclusion that the essential features of their work cannot be explained in terms of ecstatic manticism, such as became rampant in Syria and Asia Minor.

Balaam is a typical heathen diviner of a kind which

[1] *op. cit.*, p. 155

must have been familiar throughout the whole Semitic world. It should be remembered that the Biblical record of his prophecies has been fashioned and irrevocably stamped by a particular school of theology —that of believers in the sole and supreme authority of Yahwe. These theorists tended to assimilate all supernatural prophetic phenomena to the forms of ecstatic manticism which had become dominant during the monarchical period, and they possessed a clear-cut rationale with which they interpreted and justified all prophetic inspiration. The invisible, wind-like working of the *"ruach* Jehovah"—representing the extension and manifestation of God's power in the world of men—was the key-point of their rationale. In shaping the documents of the past, they imposed this theological pattern upon every piece of prophetic phenomenon. But it is possible to pierce through the outward presentation to the original constituent elements of the reality described. Thus, though the prophecies of Balaam are explicitly attributed to the inspiration of the Spirit of God, it would be a gross error to confound him with the charismatic *nabi* of later times. The narrative presupposes a wholly different circle of ideas—viz., those emanating from the realm of magic. Balaam is essentially a soothsayer such as the old Semites were accustomed to employ to help them in the business of defeating and destroying their enemies. The words of such a one were magical, poetical words, more potent than any material weapon for the sure inevitable destruction of their object. Among the Arabs, the Sha'ir was deemed to possess occult, supernaturally inspired knowledge.[1] His words not only revealed, but determined, the future: they had an objective efficacy which nothing could defeat. Ideas of this kind certainly underlie the Balaam story. Implicit in the context of events—though it would have been repudiated by those who framed the narrative—is the notion that the invincible potency of the curse sets up a real limit even to the power of God Himself. In order to check the

---

[1] Guillaume, *Prophecy and Divination*, pp. 243 ff.

disastrous consequences which would ensue from the utterance of the curse, God must prevent it from being uttered at all. The theologians who have moulded the story delight to show how Yahwe of old intervened to rescue His people from the destructive power of the curse, and how this deliverance could only be brought about by His compelling Balaam to change this deadly spell into its opposite. Another feature of the story which evinces its kinship with magic lies in the fact that the more effectively to release the curse, Balaam must mount to a height whence he can hold the people of Israel in his gaze. This points to the widespread belief among primitive peoples in the sinister effects of the evil eye. It is also connected with what we know of Semitic anthropology in general. We have seen that, for the Hebrew, psychical powers are inseparable and inconceivable apart from the physical organs through which they operate. Hence, the will to hurt and destroy, which lends potency to the magician's curse, must manifest itself through some physical channel—in this case, the eye. Furthermore, it is probable that the trance of Balaam, like that of the professional heathen *qosem*, was deliberately induced by such means as the offering of sacrifice, walking, bowing down to the earth. Finally, as Dr. Guillaume has pointed out,[1] the manner in which his prophecy was obtained—cledonomancy and the utilization of chance suggestions from objects seen—is that of Semitic divination in general. The picture of Balaam which is thus derived from these various features of the narrative presents us with a definitely characterized type, well known in the history of primitive religion. This is that of the professional diviner (*qosem*) who divines for payment (*qᵉsamim*), קסמים and whose susceptibility to inspiration is explained on the supposition that he possesses a demonic companion.

When we come to consider the character of Samuel, we are confronted by a figure who is not, as Jepsen would have us believe, the first of the spirit-possessed *nabis*, but

---

[1] *op. cit.*, p. 135

simply a representative of the old type of free Semitic diviner whose characteristic activities are proper to the conditions of nomad life. It seems that the original portrait of him as a diviner has been overlaid with representations, such as that of his leading and training the prophetic bands—which show him to be acting in quite different capacities. In what appears to be the earliest and most genuine narrative of his work (1 Sam. 9), there is no trace of that highly exalted religious emotionalism which we associate with ecstasy. He is presented simply as the possessor of occult knowledge, supernaturally inspired. He gains his secret information by a kind of mystical audition. The Lord is said to open his ear, so that he becomes capable of hearing supernatural voices which are beyond the range of normal perception (1 Sam. 9: 15). This datum accords with what we must regard as the characteristic means by which the seer, in contradistinction to the ecstatic prophet, obtains his supernatural knowledge, viz., the night-vision, in which he becomes sensitive to the whispered suggestions of a visiting demon. It is obvious that the element in Samuel's make-up which marks him out as a seer in the eyes of his contemporaries is his unerring knowledge of the future. "All that he saith cometh surely to pass" (1 Sam. 9: 6). It is just this element which the narrator revels in magnifying and elaborating. Thus, he foresees Saul's arrival in the city, the immediate purpose of his journey, and the high destiny which is in store for him. Distant events are present to him. He knows that Saul's father has left the care of the asses and has become anxious for his son's safety. He is able to predict the events, in their exact sequence, which will mark Saul's return.

Now, this uncanny intuitive knowledge surpassing the normal powers of human apprehension is something essentially different from the inspiration which accompanies the ecstatic consciousness. Predictive power is not an essential feature of states of ecstasy. The fundamental and constitutive element in such states is the merging of the human with the divine, so that man becomes a passive instrument in the hands of God. In so far as the future is revealed, it is revealed by direct self-communication on the part of the Deity, speaking through the vocal organs of the man whose personality He has seized. The typical form of experience of the *nabi*, as Jepsen has well said, is *"Gott—und Geistes Ergriffenheit"*[1] ("possession by the divine Spirit"). The typical manifestation of this subjection to overwhelming invasion by the divine is lack of self-control, disintegration, leading to glossolaly, hallucination and all the psychical phenomena which are liable to occur in unbalanced states of mind.

Now it is clear that the experience of Samuel is of quite another order. His power of probing the secrets of the future does not depend upon any psychical upheaval in the depths of his personality. The narrative suggests rather that his faculty of divination is an assured and permanent possession, and that it does not spring from passing waves of ecstatic enthusiasm such as characterized the consciousness of the genuine *nabi*. Hence we cannot agree with the interpretation of Jepsen, who sees the whole significance of Samuel in the fact that, by way of compensation for the lost ephod-oracle, he deliberately adopted the form of revelation current among the Canaanites, and thus launched the *nabi* movement in Israel.[2] The first objection to this hypothesis is that a movement of ecstatic prophesying such as is represented by the Israelite *nabis* is not something that can be consciously produced by an act of will. It is surely a singular and fundamental error to suppose, as Jepsen does, that, having lost the time-honoured oracle attached to the ark, Samuel looks around him to discover some other means of ascertaining the will of the Deity and takes over that which lies nearest to hand, viz., the enthusiastic prophesying which was rife at the Canaanite sanctuaries. Plausible and attractive as the suggestion sounds, it reposes upon an essential misunderstanding of religious phenomena. Movements of the spirit arise spontaneously, no man knows whence, and are subject to the control of

[1] *op. cit.*, p. 245   [2] *op. cit.*, pp. 111 ff.

no human agency. They can neither be fostered nor arrested, and the laws governing their working are beyond the reach of rational understanding. "The wind bloweth where it listeth. . . ." The inspiration of prophecy, like that of poetry, is a miraculous phenomenon, shrouded in mystery.

Secondly, Jepson himself admits that the tradition which makes Samuel the great initiator and prototype of the *nabis* is indeed the immediate product of the later *nabis* who cleverly traced their movement to the venerable and towering figure of Samuel as its source. He considers that the historical element in this tradition is at least that Samuel exercised his authority on behalf of the *nabis* and enabled them to win public recognition and to acquire an official and accepted status. Further, Jepsen says: "*Wieweit Samuel selbst im strengen Sinn Nabi war, wird sich mit Sicherheit kaum entscheiden lassen.*"[1] But, if Samuel was not himself a *nabi* in the fullest sense of the term, what was he? Jepsen lays emphasis upon the priestly aspect of his activities. He is a person of great importance in the city and the sacrificial meal cannot be eaten until he has blessed it. His quarrel with Saul breaks out because his prerogative in the matter of sacrifice has been infringed. Such considerations, according to Jepsen, point to the fact that Samuel was pre-eminently a priest.[2] But in the early period of Israel's history the offering of sacrifices was not a specific function of the priesthood. Sacrifices were comparatively simple. They were the normal accompaniment of certain aspects of the devotional life—the symbol and seal of pious resolution, the expression of thanksgiving and praise—and they did not require the intervention of an expert. Beyond the narrative of Samuel's youth in Shiloh, there is no evidence to suggest that he was a priest *par excellence*. Moreover, even if it were certain that Samuel was a priest, this would not be inconsistent with

[1] *op. cit.*, p. 152. "How far Samuel himself was a *nabi* in the strict sense of the word can hardly be determined with certainty"

[2] *op. cit.*, p. 110

his being a seer. On the contrary, there is a strong link between the Semitic diviner and the Semitic priest. The Hebrew word for priest is *kohen*, and the same word in Arabic (*kahin*) means diviner. The special function of the priest in primitive times is to guard the numinous shrine and its holy appurtenances, and, above all, by the manipulation of the sacred lot, to give oracles concerning the will of the Deity. He was able to make authoritative pronouncements concerning the divine will, owing to the sacredness of his person and his peculiar nearness to God. Likewise, the main task of the diviner was to ascertain the will of the gods, to reveal things hidden from mortal apprehension. In Sumero-Babylonian religion, the *baru* combined in his own person the offices of priest and diviner. By the art of hepatoscopy he was able to interpret the omens written on the quivering entrails of the animal slaughtered in sacrifice. Furthermore, attention has been drawn to the fact that we find poetic oracles attributed to the *kohens* of the tribe of Levi.[1] Now, poetry is the peculiar mark of prophetic utterance; it was thought to have been inspired by the demon who indwelt the diviner. Here then is another indication of the ancient connexion between priest and seer.

There is no sufficient reason to dismiss abruptly, with Jepsen, the hypothesis that Samuel was a seer. By doing so, Jepsen involves himself in logical difficulties, for, on the one hand, he admits that there is no convincing historical evidence that Samuel was a full-fledged *nabi*; and, on the other hand, he insists that second sight, such as Samuel undoubtedly possessed, may be ascribed to one source alone, viz., the charismatic endowment of the *nabis*.[2] To us, it seems that the figure of Samuel, with his occult knowledge and supernatural gifts, supplies just that evidence, which Jepsen desiderates, of the existence of a class of diviners and seers among the Hebrews, comparable with the Arabian *kahins* or the Babylonian *baru* priests. Moreover, in the story of the divine call

[1] Guillaume, *op. cit.*, p. 250   [2] *op. cit.*, pp. 53, 150

which came to him as a child, we have the classical instance of that night-vision which is one of the typical forms of divine communication to the seer. The essential factor in such experiences is the unseen but powerfully felt presence of a visitor from the world of gods and spirits. The communication from this world is received not through vision, but through audition. The ears of the seer are specially attuned and rendered finely sensitive to the mysterious message from within the veil. By virtue of the peculiar gift which marks him as a seer, he is able to catch the purport of the faint mutterings and whispers which denote the approach of the demon or spirit.

An excellent psychological and realistic description of such an experience is found in Job 4: 13 ff. The author stresses the fact that the presence of the divine was felt, rather than distinctly and visually perceived. The subject undergoes the characteristic reactions provoked by contact with the numinous. He is seized with terror, which exercises its appropriate physical effects on the whole bodily frame. As he crouches in silence, paralysed and overwhelmed with nervous fear, a voice becomes audible conveying thoughts which strike us at once by their inspired character—thoughts which are stamped by the authentic impress of the divine. In the case of Samuel, the divine communication takes the form of the typical prophetic oracle—a revelation of that which the Lord purposes to do and which He is announcing beforehand to the chosen servant whose ears have been specially opened that he may understand. We may note at once the close and remarkable parallel which exists between the night-vision of the seer and the special and ultimately unfathomable experience of the canonical prophet. The essence of the prophetic consciousness in both cases is the inward hearing, and spiritual assimilation of words which so deeply penetrate the soul of the prophet that he can hear them ringing with their insistent clamour through the silent spaces of the night. If we rationalize and interpret the experience in modern terms, we may say that the consciousness of the prophet is so forcibly arrested and dominated by the realization of a truth which has come to him from "out this bourne of time and space", that, for him, it has all the concrete and external objectivity of a voice audible to the physical ear. A psychical event, the whole significance of which lies in the inner realm of the spirit, externalizes itself or reflects itself in a physical sensation. Such phenomena are not unknown among the *données* of mystical experience, and the general results of modern psychological investigation confirm this interpenetration of the psychical and physical. But how much more readily intelligible becomes such a phenomenon when we realize that the Hebrew was unable to separate, in thought, even for a moment, the outer and inner, the material and spiritual worlds!

A second point which deserves to be noted and which strengthens the parallel to which we refer, is the following. Several times the great prophets speak of the Word of the Lord which came to them as something which they saw,[1] and they use the term חזה (*hazah*) which properly denotes a visual experience akin to mystical vision. How shall we explain this seemingly inappropriate use of the term? Dr. Guillaume says that "seeing and hearing are intimately bound up together", and explains the use of the term on the supposition that what the prophet hears evokes a mental image of the future which he may be said visually to perceive.[2] It remains, however, that the normal correlative of דבר (*dabar*) (in the sense of word) is שמע (*shama'*): the characteristic form of Hebrew religious experience is not mystical vision, but the obedient and trustful spirit which receives and digests the Word of the Lord. This element of spiritual communion between man and God, reposing upon a moral concord of wills, is ever central to the prophetic consciousness and reaches its culmination in Jeremiah. The characteristic type of revelation corresponding to it is the unfolding of

---

[1] e.g., the introductory notices to the prophecies of Amos, Nahum and Habbakuk
[2] *op. cit.*, p. 117

a divine purpose evoking the response of the human spirit
to meet and fulfil it. The core of the prophetic experience
is thus the hearing of a supernatural voice. Surely,
the use of חזה signifies not so much a distinct visual
impression as the historic connexion which binds the
revelation experienced by the great prophets to its crude
and dim prototype—the night-vision of the seer. In
experiences of the type exemplified by the call of
Samuel, the term חזה suggests the shuddering awareness of the divine and the reception of a supernatural
message from the beyond. "To have a vision" in this
characteristic Semitic consciousness means to be sensitive to the presence of a spirit at night, to be the recipient
of a numinous revelation. No vision is indicated, only an
auditory perception. Dr. Guillaume has pointed out that
a term for "to see" is likewise used by the Arab diviners
to denote their apprehension of a revealing omen.[1]
Evidently we are here confronted by the characteristic
Semitic mode of designating the experience of revelation
or divination proper to the seer. The retention of the
term to connote the experience of the great prophets is
an indication that some relation exists between these
latter and their ancestor—the diviner.

Another indication of the basic character and function
which Samuel possessed in the eyes of his contemporaries
is furnished by the old and reliable narrative of 1 Sam.
28. Saul, in this story, is obviously in the position of one
who wishes to consult a seer—a possessor of occult knowledge—before embarking upon a momentous under-
taking. He desires not simply to unravel the future, but
also and especially to obtain secret information as to
how he should proceed in face of the unknown. Success
in battle depends upon his being able to establish a
relationship with God, who will give him supernatural
aid, cunning in resource, and the inspiration of victory.
Here we have something parallel to the primitive
custom of having resort to the diviner, and employing his
quasi-magical powers as a potent means of obtaining

[1] *op, cit.*, p. 125

victory in warfare. It is with this clear intention that, having found the conventional means of no avail, Saul persuades the Witch of Endor to evoke the shade of Samuel. We know that, according to the prevalent religious beliefs of the time, men retained in Sheol both the dress and the function which characterized their life on earth. Thus, for Samuel to be invoked as a seer, he must have been predominantly thought of as a seer by his contemporaries. It is certainly as a seer that Saul desires to consult him. For Saul is in distress, difficulty, anxiety: he requires supernatural guidance and help. He cannot doubt that, though the prophets and dreamers of his day have failed, a seer of such towering reputation as Samuel still possesses the revelatory word, even in Sheol.[1]

Behind the figure of the Hebrew prophet, we detect not only that of the Semitic diviner, but also that of the primitive magician, the wonder-worker and rain-maker. Although the texts represent Elijah and Elisha as charismatic *nebiim*, a critical examination of their activities leads to the conclusion that they may be more truly interpreted with reference to an earlier historical type.

Elijah stands forth in sharpest contrast to the primitive professional ecstatic. Ecstatic religion is well illustrated by the priest-prophets of Baal to whom he is opposed on Mount Carmel. They are psychological experts in the art of exciting in themselves a state of mind which will automatically guarantee their union with the divine. From all such official prophetism Elijah holds himself severely aloof. It was associated in his mind with the whole system of religion which it was his life's work to combat, and from the contamination of which he set himself to rescue the worship of Yahwe. As the champion of the nomadic religion of Moses, he would find himself

[1] Other typical diviners are Deborah and Ahijah. Deborah fights for the Israelite armies by the magical potency of her prophetic word and she foretells by the use of cledonomancy. Ahijah uses the method of divination from omens. See Guillaume, *op. cit.*, pp. 139 ff.

as strenuously opposed to the deliberate employment of ecstasy as to the ritual prostitution of Yahwism.

It is not ecstasy, but the element of thaumaturgy and magic, which is prominent in Elijah.[1] He is best understood as a rain-maker, and it is not without reason that he has been identified with Al-Khidr, or the Green Man,[2] in whom the popular mind embodies the element of mystery in human life. Like Al-Khidr, Elijah springs suddenly into view fully-fledged, and does not undergo the natural process of death. He is famous as one who has power to control the weather, and he is not unnaturally blamed for the prolonged drought which afflicts the country (1 Kings 18: 17). It appears that he can command lightning to consume his enemies (2 Kings 1: 10 ff.). He is immediately recognized as a holy man through whose being there flows a current of numinous energy capable of producing supernatural effects, whether of weal or woe. The widow woman instinctively connects the sickness of her son with his disturbing presence. The awful holiness with which he is imbued is probably indicated by the title איש אלהים (*'ish 'elohim*) a title which is to be understood on the analogy of the expression בעלת אוב (*ba'alath 'ob*) and to be linked with the circles of ideas which centre around the figure of the Semitic *kahin* and his mysterious demonic companion.[3] The occult powers possessed by the man of God inhere in his very garments and impress themselves upon the instruments that he uses. The mantle of Elijah which Elisha takes up is not merely a symbol of that prophetic endowment which the former bequeaths the latter. The whole spiritual strength of the prophet has been infused into it so that the waters are miraculously divided at its touch.

[1] The prodigious physical feat involved in running before Ahab's chariot (1 Kings 18: 46) is usually considered to be an exhibition of ecstasy. But may it not be intended as a quasi-magical imitation of the oncoming storm? Even if we consider it a manifestation of ecstatic excitement, it was not deliberately provoked

[2] By Sir Richard Temple in his Presidential Address to the Jubilee Congress of the Folklore Society

[3] Hölscher, *op. cit.*, p. 127 n.

Elijah appears before his contemporaries as the rain-maker of Yahwe, and, as such, he launches a vehement attack upon the religious outlook which connected drought and rainfall with the myth of the dying and rising god. It is only from this point of view that we can properly understand the story of his controversy with the prophets of Baal. The central point of this story is Elijah's performance of a ritualistic rain charm (1 Kings 18: 33 ff). His pouring out of water is a piece of imitative magic and presupposes the idea, distinctive of this kind of magic, that like produces like. Its spiritual significance is gathered from the fact that it is done in obedience to, and in furtherance of, the will of Yahwe. It is the Yahwist's counterblast to the rain-charm which was a customary feature of the Canaanite ritual and which had as its object the securing of the *yoreh*.[1] It is done with the object of demonstrating the nonentity of the Baal or false Yahwe—the dying and rising nature-god whose features Yahwe rapidly tended to assume in popular imagination.

The element of magic and thaumaturgy becomes still more prominent in the saga relating to Elisha. Elisha is frankly a Shamanistic wonder-worker and, differing in this from his master Elijah, he seems to be an ecstatic by temperament. The significance and interest attaching to his figure reside in the fact that he combines two distinct types—the primitive medicine-man and the ecstatic prophet. On the one hand, he is shown working miracles —resurrecting the dead (even by the mere touch of his bones after his own death); multiplying and cleansing healing waters; making iron to swim (2 Kings 4: 33 ff.; 1 ff.; 42 ff.; 2 Kings 2: 19–22, 4: 38, 6: 1 ff., 13: 20 ff.). He also directs symbolic actions in a way which shows him passionately clinging to ideas proper to imitative magic (2 Kings 13: 14 ff.); he uses cledonomancy (2 Kings 7). On the other hand, he foresees future events (2 Kings 8: 12); pierces the secret intent of the heart (2 Kings 6: 12); divines what is taking place at a distance

[1] Hooke, *Origins of Early Semitic Ritual*, p. 35

47

(2 Kings 6: 32) by means of abnormal psychic power which we associate with ecstatic prophecy. He employs music as a means of inducing the prophetic mood (2 Kings 3: 15). Here we see the primitive tradition of magic and divination becoming associated with the psychic phenomena of ecstasy, and so issuing in the complex character of the Hebrew prophetic consciousness.

Such were the predecessors of the Hebrew prophets. We have now to trace the continuing activity of this ancient tradition of Semitic divination and magic as a formative element in the consciousness of those prophets themselves.

This tradition is manifested in the prophetic conception of the spoken word and the acted sign. That understanding of the uttered word which determines the role of the Semitic diviner moulds the prophet's belief concerning the significance and efficacy of his oracles. Both the prophet and his contemporaries believe the declared Word of prophecy to be a mysterious entity which cannot fail to fulfil itself in the outward embodiment of event. It not only reveals but effectually determines the shape of things to come. Hence, it excites awe and fear in the hearers. Hosea and Isaiah attach to their children names which are fraught with a terrible and creative significance. Jeremiah is told that the divine words which have been placed in his mouth are to be the efficacious instruments whereby he will have power to sway the destinies of empires (Jer. 1: 9, 10). In another passage, it is revealed to him that the words of God in his mouth will become a fire to consume the people (5: 14). Again, in Jer. 23: 29, the destructive potency of the Word is compared to a hammer which shatters the rock. The woeful soul-shaking words of Amos are unendurable to his countrymen (Amos 7: 10); and, according to Hos. 6: 5, the divine words spoken by the prophets are the means by which Yahwe brings death and destruction to His people. This idea is enforced by the crude realism with which it is expressed: Yahwe is said to hew and slay by means of His Word. The word of Jeremiah both announces and effects the death of Hananiah (Jer. 28: 17), in the same way that the prophesying of Ezekiel brings about the death of Pelatiah (Ezek. 11: 13).

These examples make it abundantly clear that the prophets work with the ancient quasi-magical conception of the Word as an unquenchable independent energy which must produce the effects proper to it. This conception, emanating from the circle of ideas connected with divination and magic, is reinforced by the pre-suppositions of current Hebrew psychology. The breath-soul, conceived as the totality of the psycho-physical life, pours itself out into all its material manifestations, impregnating with its essence even the clothes which a man wears. The spoken word is the instrument with which the soul realizes itself and exercises a creative influence on other souls. To speak a word, for the Hebrew consciousness, is to introduce a new potentiality into the stream of historical events. Now, if such is the decisive importance which the Hebrew attaches to the spoken word of man, *a fortiori* the word in the mouth of the prophet which is believed to be the Word of God Himself will naturally be considered as a determining creative factor in the making of history. The divine Word declared by the prophets will be regarded as the most palpable evidence of the unfailing operation of the divine energy in the final ordering of history.

The acted sign is imbued with the same potent signi-ficance as the spoken word, and illustrates yet more vividly the persistent influence of magical conceptions in the development of the Hebrew prophetic consciousness. In its formal aspect, the acted sign is undoubtedly a pro-longation of imitative magic and is to be interpreted on the same lines as Elijah's performance of rain-making ceremonies. Its vital import is missed if we regard it merely as an elaborate dramatic illustration calculated to impress the childlike imagination of the prophet's contemporaries. It is much more even than an example of the process of ritualistic representation by which primitive man dances out the beliefs of his heart. It is now generally accepted that the acted sign not only adumbrated in miniature the eventual fulfilment of the Word, but was conceived in the most realistic fashion as making an effectual contribution towards that process of fulfilment itself. The proof of this assertion lies in the fact that such signs were sometimes performed without witness and sometimes preceded in time the oracles to which they referred. Again, the seriousness with which the sign was regarded is clear from the story of Jeremiah's encounter with Hananiah. The latter considers that a mere verbal refutation of the prophet is not enough. In order to guard against the deadly fulfilment of Jeremiah's words he must shatter the sign and thus frustate the fulfilment which it would otherwise have. When Ezekiel at the divine command portrays the image of a beleaguered city upon a tile, or laboriously enacts the drama of a panic-stricken flight from home; when Jeremiah breaks the potter's vessel or buries stones in Egypt; when Isaiah walks barefooted for three years; he is conscious of exercising a power over events, of hastening the process by which the purpose of Yahwe will be fulfilled. Only on this assumption can the earnest deliberation and the childlike faith with which these actions are performed become intelligible to us.

But the prophet, while continuing the methods of the magician, transforms them by making them the vehicle of a religious consciousness. The prophet acts in obedience and self-surrender to the declared will of Yahwe. He clings with passionate personal adherence to that will and by his symbolic actions believes that he promotes its realization. The magician, on the contrary, acts in independence of, and is indifferent to, the will of God. His mimetic acts are the private manipulation of reality for the satisfaction of personal desire. The acted sign of the prophet is the pledge of his loving self-identification with his God: the act of the magician is a defiant coercion of God.

This interpretation of prophetic symbolism is in harmony with the general metaphysical implications of

the Hebrew approach to life. For the Hebrew, there is
no antithesis between the outward and the inward, the
physical and the psychical, the material and the spiritual.
Just as those concepts which we regard as essentially
spiritual, e.g., sin and holiness, are materialistically conceived, so material things are penetrated with divine
meaning, and the universe of Hebrew man becomes
pregnant with spiritual significance. The Semite inhabits
a world in which the sleepless activity of God is believed
to determine occurrences which we should explain on
other grounds. No external event is a loose, detached
portion of reality: it coheres with a larger whole from
which it derives its meaning. The symbolic act is envisaged solely with reference to the psychic context with
which it is indissolubly united. It is embedded in the
very stuff of reality and guarantees the realization of that
whole from which it cannot be detached. Nothing that
happens to the prophet in his personal life is without a
deep esoteric significance. Hosea in his marriage,
Jeremiah in his celibacy, Ezekiel in the death of his
wife, see so many Words uttering the divine passion or
shadowing forth the divine purpose.

This analysis leads to the conclusion that the Hebrew
prophetic consciousness represents the spiritual flowering
of the native Semitic tradition of divination, and a
religious transformation of widespread primitive magic.
The prophets entertain towards their words and actions
a complex of beliefs which can be explained on no other
hypothesis. The external, formal, mechanism through
which their prophecies are mediated is that of normal
Semitic divination, whether it be divination from the
observation of omens, from assonance, from a chance
utterance, or from the deep metaphysical significance of
an external event. But, behind the continuity of outward
form and technique, there lies a sharp cleavage between
the prophet and the diviner. The one is dominated and
possessed by his God, and prophesies in response to a
divine initiative which exercises over him an irresistible
control. Although, in becoming the mouth of God, the

prophet's personality is not dissolved in union with the divine, yet his prophetic consciousness arises solely out of his reaction to the prevenient activity of God. He is a prophet, not because he has been initiated into the secrets of a particular technique, but because he is conscious of having received a divine commission. The diviner, on the other hand, exercises his divinatory technique independently of any religious experience. His divination springs from his own personal initiative; he is subject to no divine control from the outside. The demonic companion is conceived as an impersonal voice rather than as a spiritual energy; the whispered suggestions which float through the darkness are an objectification of the inspired inner ego of the diviner.

The religious transformation effected by the prophetic consciousness is reached through the re-orientation of this Semitic tradition by vitalizing contact with the ecstatic movement of Syria. The restless, nomadic Israelites were thus brought into touch with a wave of infectious spiritual enthusiasm which they assimilated to their native religious culture and psychology. The frenzied, God-intoxicated, nabi is regarded as being controlled by the invasive ruach of Yahwe. But the point we are most concerned to emphasize is that in the ecstatic phenomena of the land of Canaan they were first introduced to a form of manticism which produced a supernatural change in the personality of the prophet and effectively united him to the divine which entered into him and employed his vocal organs. Under the invasive touch of the god, the subject of ecstasy himself became god. While this notion of deification must have been repugant to the Hebrew, with his emphasis upon the infinite distance between Creator and creature, the type of experience which underlies it undoubtedly entered as an element into the making of the Hebrew prophetic consciousness. In the next chapter, we shall see how the religious experience of ecstasy, as well as the mechanism of divination, is given a new significance as it is taken up into the sphere of Hebrew theology and psychology.

Chapter Two

PROPHETIC VISION AND ECSTASY
IN THE LIGHT OF HEBREW PSYCHOLOGY

(i)

IN the Book of Numbers we have a passage which suggests that dream and vision were recognized as the normal medium through which God conveyed His message to the mind of the prophet (Num. 12: 6). From Jeremiah's controversy with the false prophets, we learn that these psychic experiences were assiduously cultivated in a way which implies that they formed part of a definite mantic technique. It is surely a mistake to seek to eliminate the visionary element from the consciousness of the great prophets themselves. "I saw the Lord" is a phrase which is used not only by Micaiah, but also by Amos and Isaiah, and which denotes some kind of supernormal ecstatic experience (Amos 9: 1, Isaiah 6: 1). Once the prophet has received the call to prophesy, there breaks forth upon his consciousness the vision of an unseen and glorious world interpenetrating and transfiguring the prosaic world of everyday. He is equipped with psychical gifts befitting his office. Isaiah, rapt in ecstatic meditation in the sanctuary at Jerusalem, is crushed by the dreadful majesty of the Ancient of Days: Ezekiel feels that the heavens are opened and that he is permitted to behold a dazzling epiphany in storm, lightning, and tempest. Or the same divine working empowers the prophet to envision the realization of that which at present lies concealed in the womb of souls and to influence events taking place at a distance. The Hebrew prophet cannot wholly escape the influence of the ecstatic phenomena with which he is confronted in Palestine, but he imparts to these unusual psychic states a new significance by interpreting them in accordance with the implicates of his own special psychology and theology.

In the Semitic world-view, events are understood to exist primarily and fundamentally in the soul of the doer. The Hebrew does not distinguish between intention and result. An action, the import of which is not realized by the agent, is not thereby robbed of its significance as a revealer of the soul. Jonathan cannot be relieved of the responsibility for the deed which he performed unwittingly. The outward action must correspond to, and make manifest, an inner psychic reality from which it proceeds. For the Hebrew prophet, dream and vision represent the revelation of those underlying spiritual realities which determine the complex play of events. Dreams are significant because in them we see a future reality already reacting upon the soul of the dreamer. The dreams of Joseph are revealing because they could only have sprung from the soul of a ruler. The events which they portend are already firmly planted in his soul and must eventually be realized outwardly. It is for this reason that they excite the anger and hostility of his brethren and call forth the rebuke of his father for the arrogance that they imply.

There is no reason to make any fundamental distinction between dream and vision, except the obvious one that they belong respectively to the experiences of sleeping and waking. Both are a revelation of the heart of reality and their truth arises from the penetrating sureness and depth of the prophets' knowledge of souls. The true prophet, as distinguished from the false, is he whose vision can penetrate to the hidden laws of reality, the hidden pattern of the soul's life. It is the prophet's insight into the spirit-world which lends truth and significance to any ecstatic experience that he may have. The true vision is a process of inner spiritual seeing and is possible only to him whose eye the Lord has opened. The future is seen as the fulfilment of something immanent in the context of the present.

Both Micaiah and his opponents[1] are governed by a type of inspiration which can only be described as

[1] 1 Kings 22

ecstatic. But the ecstasy is a psychical form which cannot guarantee the truth of its content. Micaiah is the true visionary because he sees in the heart of Ahab's personal character the antecedents of the defeat to which he will succumb. His power to prophesy truly springs from his grasp of the spiritual context to which the future event integrally belongs.

Elisha again is an example of an ecstatic visionary whose far-reaching insight penetrates the barriers of space and time. He has such a vital understanding of souls as enables him to divine the outcome of their present state. This is vividly illustrated by the story of his dramatic encounter with Hazael.[1] As the prophet gazes steadfastly upon him and penetrates to the heart of his being, he sees a picture of the future which to him is as intensely and objectively real as are the sense impressions of everyday life.

Most of the visions of Amos were reached along the lines of Semitic divination from omens. But the age-old mechanism of divination is transformed by the power of spiritual vision which is the peculiar endowment of the Hebrew prophet. The primary importance of vision in the prophetic consciousness of Amos is suggested in the introductory notice to his prophecies. "The words of Amos . . . which he saw concerning Israel." The title of the book might fittingly be paraphrased "Things seen." The starting-point for the vision is some object of everyday experience—a basket of summer fruit, locusts devouring grass, the fierce midsummer heat, the assembled worshippers in the shrine at Bethel—but the vision itself is something which transcends the common spectacle, something which moves, as it were, in a new dimension of reality concealed from the common gaze. As the prophet's eye broods upon the physical object, there flashes upon his inward sight the startling, terrifying, vision of the deep spiritual realities which it suggests. It is easy enough to interpret the experience from a modern standpoint and to show that, humanly

[1] 2 Kings 8: 9 ff.

speaking, it is a phenomenon which arises from association—the association of an everyday object with the spiritual content of the prophet's meditations. Needless to say, the prophet did not interpret his experience thus, nor would he have understood the distinction made by the modern psychologist and theologian between internal and external seeing. For him, with his fusion of the physical and the psychical, the inspired insight into spiritual truth is in some way included within the experience of physical vision; the physical eye itself—in a manner which we cannot understand because we cannot recapture the primitive anthropology—becomes the instrument which in the hands of God mediates the knowledge of the divine will.

Perhaps the best example of Amos' power of seeing beyond the immediate object to the spiritual context and the future event which this implies is afforded by the last vision in the recorded cycle. We may suppose him to have mingled with the worshippers who at the season of the great festivals thronged the famous sanctuary at Bethel. As he lets his gaze fall upon the altar with its bull-images and all the apparatus of its luxuriant ritual, his fascinated vision, informed by his burning moral indignation and his clear-sighted apprehension of the truth, discovers there the figure of Yahwe to whom this worship is addressed. At last, Yahwe's fierce aversion to the immoralities committed in His name, translates itself into violent action. The prophet sees Yahwe destroy the altar with the people gathered around it. Unfortunately, the text is corrupt, but it is probable that originally the action was represented as completed (וַיַּךְ (vayak) instead of the imperative הַךְ (hak)). The psychological mechanism determining the vision is that which we have already outlined and illustrated. The prophet's penetrating judgment has appraised the worth of this mechanical ritualistic worship and has realized the repugnance which it excites in Yahwe. Then, as he gazes with contemplative vision upon the external objects of the scene, he sees through time to the event which can be the only logical outcome of those inner spiritual realities which he has laid bare.

Ezekiel is the prophetic visionary *par excellence*: his personality was of that type which has been denominated "mediumistic". We may conjecture that he was more subject to abnormal psychoses, and fell more easily into ecstatic trance than any other of the great prophets. Our interpretation of the prolonged visionary experience which we find recorded in Chapters 8–11 will depend largely upon the view which we take as to the literary composition of his book as a whole. If we suppose that the exilic framework was supplied by a later hand, then the account of the prophet's ecstatic soul-voyage from Babylonia to Jerusalem is a mere literary fiction devised to present the material in the setting of the Exile. It cannot be denied that there is *Lebenswahrheit* and a note of dramatic realism in the narrative of the prophet's being shown the iniquitous cult-practices of the Temple. Also, the account in Chapter 11 reads as if Pelatiah's death were a direct consequence of the prophetic word. The discussion of this problem from the literary stand-point lies outside our subject, but we may note that there is no absolute psychological impossibility in the narrative as it stands. According to Hebrew psychology, the soul is an elastic complex of forces which can extend its power through space as well as time. No soul lives to itself: all the souls within a psychic group interpenetrate and react upon each other, and the power of the soul to influence other souls with whom it is in vital contact is not wholly limited by space. The prophet especially, in whom the human breath-soul is dominated by an irruption of the divine energy, can project his soul through space. This must not be understood in the sense that the soul, as if it were an independent entity, leaves the body, but rather in the sense that the heightened spiritual consci-ousness of the prophet, whether concentrated in the eye or ear, bursts the bounds of time and space which would normally limit its action. Just as Elisha can hear the words which the King of Syria speaks in his bedchamber, so Ezekiel in Babylon can see the wickedness perpetrated in the Temple at Jerusalem, and can exert an influence upon the souls with whom he is in contact there. It is the very nature of souls thus to penetrate and creatively influence other souls; and, in the higher reaches of consciousness, not even the limits of space can check the expansion of these inspired energies of the soul.

The starting-point for Ezekiel's visions in ecstatic trance is his intense mental preoccupation with the blasphemous wickedness of the inhabitants of Jerusalem. Prior to his exile, he has seen with his bodily eyes the heathen idolatries which now desecrate God's sanctuary, and his whole soul is convulsed within him as he realizes the offence which this has caused to the majesty and holiness of the transcendent God. An exile in Babylon, his heart is in Jerusalem and his attention is rapt in contemplation of its evil, and of the fierce wrath of God, at last about to burst forth upon and consume a faithless people. Such an intense concentration of attention is sufficient to excite the trance-state, and there surges up before him in visual, objective form, as though from some source outside himself, those vivid images which memory supplies and which now stand out with such luminous clarity that he believes himself to be living and moving at the very spot to which his vision relates. This psychological interpretation would surely adequately explain the almost startling *Lebenswahrheit* and realism of the narrative. On psychological grounds, it is not at all necessary to have recourse to the supposition that the original version consisted merely in an account of an experience which took place at Jerusalem.

In the second and third visions of the execution of divine vengeance and Yahwe's abandonment of His sanctuary, we see how the slowly ripened fruit of the prophet's meditations, his profound insight into the laws which govern the spiritual world, are externalized and translated into the form of objective vision. Gazing in dream-like trance, he sees actually taking place those future events implied in a spiritual situation which has burnt itself into the heart of his inmost being.

It is of the highest importance to point out that while it is possible to reconstruct, from a naturalistic standpoint, the psychological mechanism which underlies the form of this experience, its one and only source, from a theological standpoint, is the divine initiative. As in the case of Amos, the Lord takes possession of the personality of Ezekiel and causes him to see supernatural visions. He is transported to Jerusalem under the compulsion of the divine spirit. The otherness of that which determines the whole experience is particularly strongly emphasized.

The same transcendent compelling Power initiates and determines the vision of the resurrected bones. Here, again, the fact that the prophet in his ecstatic vision is under the driving constraint of the divine Spirit is made abundantly explicit in the text. We must not suppose that the vision is simply a literary fiction or parable designed to illustrate the truth that the exiled people will be miraculously restored and resurrected to a new life in the spirit. We should rather see in it an acted sign which God Himself performs as a token and guarantee of the marvellous resurrection with which He purposes to recreate the life of the nation. The resurrection of the bones at the command of the Word of God is but a concrete and palpable manifestation in miniature of that all-powerful divine *ruach* which can engender the spiritual regeneration of a whole people. The former necessarily implies the latter and is therefore a token ensuring the realization of the latter. Through long years of meditation the conviction has been slowly borne in upon the prophet's mind that Yahwe's nature and being are such that He cannot allow His people wholly to perish: the first Israel which has been destroyed will be succeeded by one spiritually revitalized and fitted to accomplish the divine purpose. Then, one day, with a consciousness enhanced and quickened by the coercive sway of the divine Spirit, this brooding conviction is translated into terms of ecstatic vision. Doubtless his attention became absorbed by the contemplation of the actual dry bones, until physical sight was swallowed up in spiritual illumination, until "the light of sense went out, but with a flash that had revealed the invisible world".

(ii)

We shall now turn to consider the Biblical evidence for the peculiar psychological characteristics of the prophetic consciousness and shall interpret this in the light of our study of Hebrew psychology and anthropology.

According to the statements of the prophets themselves, the distinguishing feature of their experience is the sense of compulsion under which they speak. It is the feeling of *Ergriffensein von der göttlichen Macht* ("The being seized by the divine power").[1] The constantly repeated formula *Ko amar Yahwe* expresses their consciousness of the otherness and objectivity of their message. It springs from a source outside themselves. The prophet is passive. The message which he is compelled to utter presses upon him from without. It takes shape before him as an insistent overwhelming cry thundering in his ears and forcing him to speak (Isa. 5: 9; 22: 14). This sense of irresistible divine pressure is expressed in the phrase יד יהוה (*yad Jehovah*). Ezekiel at the time of his initiatory vision is conscious of being overpowered by the strong hand of the Lord (3: 15, 22). Isaiah says: "Yahwe spake thus to me with strength of hand" (בחזקת היד) (*b⁼ haz⁼qath ha yad*) (8: 11). Amos asserts that his prophecy proceeds from the logic of cause and effect; it is grounded in the objective self-revelation of Yahwe (Amos 3: 8). Jeremiah, with his tendency to lyrical *épanchement*, has allowed us to glimpse something of the inner painful conflict to which his call to prophesy gives rise. He shrinks abashed and fearful before the magnitude of the task that is thrust upon him. He struggles to evade the responsibilities and the burden of the prophetic office. Unlike the professional ecstatic, he does not seek to cultivate the

---

[1] Lindblom, *Die literarische Gattung der prophetischen Literatur*, Uppsala, 1924, p. 42

presence of God; rather, he sinks overwhelmed at this formidable confrontation by the demands of the divine will (Chapter 1). The compulsive urge to prophesy presents itself as a divine intrusion upon his personality. It provokes a psychic upheaval in the depths of his soul-life. The delicate balance of his normal consciousness is completely overthrown. In one passage (4: 19 ff.), he tells how his being is convulsed with anguish, physical and mental, under the oppression of the blasting vision of destruction which obsesses his gaze; he cannot hold his peace, so mighty is the sway of the divine *ruach*. In another passage, he speaks of himself as being so full of the fury of the Lord that his self-restraint breaks down (6: 11). The idea is that of a power other than himself which holds him in its grip and compels him to utterance. He staggers, as the divine spirit invades and masters his soul. His heart is broken, his bones shake, he is like one overcome with wine (23: 9). Most revealing of all is the famous dialogue between his soul and Yahwe reported in Chapter 20: 7 ff., from which it appears that, if he represses the revelation, then it becomes a torturing presence within him—a fire burning in his bones and forcing the barriers of his soul.

A characteristically Hebrew description of the psychic disturbance which may accompany the prophetic consciousness is found in Isa. 21. Here the sense of being gripped by an overpowering, invading, presence becomes so intense that the prophet experiences a violent disruption of his personality. The spiritual force *ab extra*, by which he is inspired, stands out and is objectified over against the prophet's more normal consciousness. It becomes the watchman or the ecstatic seer whose piercing vision can penetrate space and time and behold events as yet unrealized. But this division of personality by the invading divine spirit does not take place without provoking convulsive disturbances in the prophet's soul and body. It is especially significant that this psychic agitation expresses itself in physical changes which shake and distort the whole bodily frame. The loins (מתן)

are racked with pains comparable to those of child-birth: the body becomes so distorted (עות) that the subject can neither see nor hear: the heart reels (תעה) as a result of this powerful disturbance of the soul's poise.

The hand of the Lord acts as a kind of hypnotic force, provoking somnambulistic movements. This is especially the case with Ezekiel, who, in the stress of his inspiration, wanders from place to place much like a sleepwalker. After his first visionary experience he is represented as going to the dwelling-place of the exiles under the suggestive compulsion of his "ecstatic" mood. It is clear that his consciousness has become so narrowed and concentrated that he has partially lost self-control: he is driven onwards by a force other than himself (3: 14, 15). At another time, the hypnotic pressure of the hand of the Lord takes the form of a command bidding him go out into the valley, where he receives a revelation in ecstasy (3: 22 ff.). In 37: 1, 2, however, the divine pressure is pictured as physical power which transports him bodily from place to place.

If we would interpret this sense of possession in accordance with the *données* of Hebrew psychology, we must begin with the Hebrew conception of man as a being who is conspicuously accessible to demonic invasion from without. Hence, it is most natural to explain the prophetic sense of compulsion as the violent irruption into the prophet's soul of the divine *ruach*. It is continuous with the Israelite tradition of the manner in which Yahwe's spirit operates among men. The essential feature of such operation is that it is productive of mysterious, otherwise inexplicable, effects and that it dominates and overwhelms the soul upon which it is performed. The man upon whom the Spirit leaps is supernaturally transfigured. He becomes another man. Thenceforth, he lives in the power of the Spirit and is urged and emboldened to act in a way which is contrary to his habitual nature and transcends the limit of his natural capacities. Thus, the Judges are raised up and equipped with divine strength to overthrow Israel's oppressor. Thus we read that, when Saul turned to go away from Samuel, God gave him another heart (1 Sam. 10: 8): in token of this radical change the divine *ruach* rushes upon him and he "prophesies". The eccentric gestures which accompanied his ecstatic state proceeded from the divine power which was mastering his soul, just as much as did the superhuman strength and authority which enabled him to defeat the Ammonites. His whole personality is manifesting itself in quite a new way because he has submitted to the intrusive control of the Spirit of God.

Similarly, madness, disease, obsession, simply because they are abnormal and defy explanation in terms of nature, are ascribed to the invasive force of the *ruach* of Yahwe. The political obtuseness of the Egyptians is so extraordinary that it can only be understood on the supposition of its being due to a spirit of perverseness sent by Yahwe (Isa. 19: 14). The mental disease of Saul and the ecstatic inspiration of the prophet are ascribed to the same source (1 Sam. 16: 14–16; 18: 10; 19: 9; 10: 6, 10; 19: 20, 23; 1 Kings 22: 24; Hos. 9: 7).

This interpretation of the prophetic consciousness springs inevitably from the Hebrew conception of the human soul and the divine *ruach*, and is sharply differentiated from the Greek conception of εκστασις.[1] For the Hebrew the soul is no fixed entity, seeking to realize its inherent divinity by becoming re-united with its divine source. So far from bearing a constant nature and pattern, it is plastic material which is being continuously fashioned by its Maker that it may the more adequately respond to His purposes. It is a vast deep reservoir of latent potentialities, finely sensitive to the touch of the divine Spirit. Behind the conscious soul—a norm artificially adapted to the requirements of the everyday world—there lies this penumbra of infinite and mysterious depth which may at any moment be invaded

---

[1] i.e., literally, a being put out of its place—the transportation of the soul, in mystical rapture, outside its bodily prison

by the divine and from which there surges with vivid objectivity the vision and audition which frequently accompany prophetic experience. This explosion of the divine in the hidden depths of the soul's life effects that wondrous change of personality which marks out the inspired prophet and leader from his fellows. The divine energy thrusts itself intrusively into his soul, filling it with a new rich content and endowing it with unusual gifts. The prophet is no longer master of his own soul, which is made subservient to and controlled by the divine. This movement is the opposite of that which characterizes the ecstasy of the Greeks, who begin with the conception of the incarnate soul and suppose that by strenuous self-cultivation it bursts its carnal fetters, achieving an enlarged consciousness in which it realizes its union with the divine.

In using the notion of the *ruach* as the key with which to interpret the prophetic sense of possession, the one difficulty which confronts us is that the canonical prophets, with the exception of Ezekiel, never explicitly refer to the divine Spirit as the source of their inspiration. This omission is the more striking in that it contrasts with the current theological rationale which explains the ecstatic prophesying of the earlier *nebiim* by attributing it to the invasion of the Spirit of Yahwe. But the omission has not the decisive significance which Jepsen ascribes to it. It is true, however, that the great prophets feel so acutely the vital difference which separates them from their professional brethren that they instinctively abstain from using the accepted explanation of prophecy. Doubtless this explanation is associated in their minds with mere *Raserei*—psychic abnormality unrelated to the deliverance of a revealed message. In their own consciousness, the upheaval of personality which accompanies the sense of divine coercion is organically connected with the vision of the Word. This would explain their reserve. To their minds, the inner essence of their peculiar consciousness is shrouded in mystery. It is most naturally interpretable in terms of the psychology with which they are familiar, yet it is not wholly reducible to a mechanical formula.

This nuance does not affect the main issue, which is already decided by the fact that the prophet claims to prophesy (*hithnabbe*) in the name of the Lord. This means that his message—even though we should regard it as the product of normal reflective processes of thought—is by the prophet himself attributed wholly to Yahwe. But in what sense did the prophet consider himself to be speaking the words of Yahwe? How did he conceive the divine message to have been conveyed to his consciousness? The prophet could only have answered these questions in terms of the current psychology. He cannot have shared in that psychology without allowing it to influence his own conception of his personality and of its relation to Yahwe. Seeing that he believed his message to have sprung from a divine source outside himself, he must also have believed that in conceiving the message his mind was working under the controlling authority and guidance of the divine. The message was the result of the divine life or spirit operating with explosive effects in his own consciousness. The prophet could have imagined such a process only on the lines we have indicated, only through the presuppositions of Hebrew psychology with its twin conceptions of the human flesh-soul and the divine *ruach*. The flash of inspiration in which the message is born implies the working of the divine within the human consciousness; and it is just such an operation of the divine at the heart of created life which the idea of the *ruach* is used to denote. The operation of the *ruach*, however, does not effect a deification of the soul but signifies rather the divine creative energy quickening and transforming the human. It represents the *continuous* creative act of God.

Hence, it must not be supposed that the divine *ruach* temporarily displaces the fleshly breath-soul of the prophet. Such a supposition would be unthinkable, since the life of the prophet inheres in his breath-soul which constitutes him an individual person. If we would understand the prophetic consciousness aright, we have to see that the prophet, when most fully inspired, is most fully possessed of the use of his human faculties. The divine *ruach* is not a substance which, in order to force an entry into the prophet's personality, must oust one of its constituent elements. It should be conceived as the power and energy of God—invisible and wind-like—under the impact of which the prophet's integrated psychophysical life is wrought to the highest pitch of intensified and concentrated consciousness.

This interpretation of the way in which the *ruach* is related to the human personality of the prophet is confirmed by the consideration that prophetic inspiration can be mediated through one or other of the physical organs. The prophet is not rapt beyond himself into some mystic empyrean. His inspiration springs from the divine use of the natural and physiological. His personality, consisting in a consciousness diffused through a number of harmoniously co-operating physical parts, is ever open to receive wonderful new accessions of life as it comes under the touch of the divine breath. Since consciousness may be temporarily localized in some one physical organ, the enhanced perceptiveness and insight, imparted by divine quickening, may also be mediated through one particular sense-activity. Only on this hypothesis can we explain the enormously important part played by sense-impressions in suggesting the spiritual nucleus of the revelation. The thinking of the prophet is inextricably interwoven with his sensuous life. The divine control of his consciousness becomes the divine control of his physiological impressions. The simplicity and unity of the primitive mentality is never dissolved. There is no divorce between outward and inward, physical and psychical, action and thought. Jeremiah, walking abroad when all nature is wrapped in wintry sleep, suddenly finds himself looking steadily at the ever-watchful almond-tree. The contrast between the unfailingly flourishing tree and the dead landscape around releases into consciousness a train of thought which hitherto had been buried in the unconscious layers of his mind. The prophet's faith is that it is his God who has inspired and controlled the act of visual perception in order to convey thereby to the prophet's mind the truth concerning the divine purpose and character. The common object which bears no particular meaning to the unseeing eye, and is but one of a multitude of objects that are for ever surging upon the senses of man, stands forth to the prophet invested with mystic light, arresting his vision and arousing in him an understanding of the divine will. Almost all the visionary experiences of the prophets are to be interpreted in this way. These visions do not represent the conscious use of literary symbolism, nor are they the product of the mind which, no longer subject to intelligent self-control, combines in arbitrary dream-like fashion the images stored in the memory. Both of these explanations are characteristically modern, and both fail to do justice to that which is central and essential in the prophetic experience, viz., the divine use of sensuous activity. The principle that the realization of divine truth may be mediated through the groping and striving of human experience is one which is familiar and acceptable to modern thought, but what does strike us as strange is that this revealing experience should embrace the physical as well as the psychical aspect of human life. For us, the spiritual consciousness—the life of feeling and thought—seems to be abstracted from the realm of bodily sensation. We have lost irrecoverably the indivisible wholeness and integration which characterized the personality of primitive man. But we have seen that, for the Hebrew, the psychical is unknown apart from the physical centres through which it is manifested. His thinking is never divorced from his manifold sensation. Hence, the revelation of the divine through the human resolves itself into the divine control of the prophet's sense-activity. The great key-points of the prophetic message are flashed upon the prophet's consciousness from the aroma of spiritual suggestiveness which gathers round his visual perceptions.

67

The diffusion of consciousness through the various physical organs enables the prophet the more easily to conceive the idea that in its inspired state his personality is being subjected to the invasion of the divine *ruach*. Since his personality is understood to be a well-organized multiplicity of parts, he was led to detach and externalize that part of himself believed to be the special means by which God took possession of his soul. This is especially the case in regard to the prophet's mouth, which was identified with the mouth of Yahwe in the most naïve and realistic fashion. The prophet was the mouthpiece of God, as truly as Aaron was the mouthpiece of Moses. It was by controlling and employing the prophet's mouth that the divine *ruach* entered into and dominated his personality. The seriousness with which this conception was entertained is made clear from the accounts of the inaugural visions of Isaiah and Jeremiah. The purification of Isaiah's lips shows the inseparability of physical and spiritual in the Hebrew view of man. The sin which corrupts the soul *ipso facto* corrupts the flesh through which the soul must express itself and apart from which the soul has no meaning and no existence. From the standpoint of inspired prophetic utterance, it is the mouth and lips in which the soul-life inheres and it is they which must therefore be cleansed. The same significance attaches to the solemn action in which Yahwe's hand is outstretched to touch Jeremiah's mouth. This is not a poetic metaphor expressing spiritual truth. It is as realistically understood that the words of God are placed in the prophet's mouth as that Ezekiel eats and digests the sacred roll on which his woeful oracles are inscribed. The formula *Ko amar Yahwe* is one which this particular psychological interpretation of his deepest spiritual experience compels him to employ. It is singularly unscientific and unhistorical to suppose, as is sometimes done, that the use of such a phrase necessarily implies a mystical ecstatic audition. It is more natural to consider that its use is determined by the psychological assumptions characteristic of the prophet's age. Given the widespread belief in the peculiar accessibility of human nature to invasion from without; given also the unforgettable character of the prophet's initial experience of a call; it is easy to understand that he would tend to rank as objective inspiration states of mind—insight, spiritual vision, dramatic imagination—which modern Western man would ascribe to sources within himself. We must also remember that the Hebrew was quite unable to distinguish the abstract from the concrete, the soul from the body. He would have been simply incapable of such a feat of metaphysical dexterity as is involved in supposing that the deepest convictions of his own mind and heart had eternal validity, were the eternal thought of God refracting itself through the medium of the human spirit. He was obliged to cast the interpretation of his experience into the thought-forms common to his age, and to express his conviction of the validity of his message by describing it as the very Word of God.

Chapter Three

THE WRITING PROPHETS AND THE *NEBIIM*

IN the preceding chapter, it has been pointed out that the canonical prophets fail to give explicit sanction to the reigning theory of prophetic inspiration. In this reserve we may detect their implicit desire to guard themselves from too close an identification with the professional *nebiim*. Hence arises the problem of their exact relationship to the latter. We find indeed that almost every one of the great prophets is locked in deadly and bitter conflict with the official representatives of their class. They are solitary individuals of such towering originality as to transcend and differentiate themselves from the type out of which they emerge. In the flowering of their genius they burst the framework to which they might seem to belong, and we see in them the rise of something new and qualitatively distinct from its antecedents. Amos, the first of their number, indignantly repudiates the suggestion that he is a *nabi*, as though he considered it derogatory (7: 14 ff.). The passage implies that by this time the exercise of a call to prophesy had become an official profession, to which remuneration was attached and had secured a recognized, though perhaps not an admired, status in the community. In answer to the charge of the high priest, Amos refers proudly to his agricultural vocation, which automatically precludes his association with the *nebiim*. He seems anxious to stress his economic independence, from which it would appear that the *nebiim* had to rely upon the miserably exiguous recompense which they were offered for their prophetic counsel. Hosea opens up a violent polemic against the ritual system of his day in which prophet as well as priest is implicated (4: 4 ff.). This close association of prophet and priest indicates the

extent to which the Canaanite religious system had corrupted and perverted the native Mosaic religion of
Israel. Prophet, priest and people all alike stumble for
lack of knowledge: whoredom and wine have fuddled
their understanding. This polemic is continued and intensified by Micah, Isaiah and Jeremiah. Micah passionately affirms his own immediate certainty of knowing
God and as passionately denounces the criminal blindness, self-seeking and stupidity in which the official
prophets are engulfed. By their own sin they are cut
off from the knowledge of God and therefore cannot
divine truly (3: 5 ff.). Indeed, so incredibly depraved are
the prophets that *ruach*, the very hall-mark of divine
inspiration, is now linked with falsehood (שקר, *shakar*),
as if cause and effect (Mic. 2: 11). Such are the prophets
whom the people fervently acclaim. The irony of the
situation is emphasized by Jeremiah. The ecstatic spirit-
possession of the prophets is so completely devoid of
inner spiritual significance and content that Jeremiah
can make a play on the word *ruach*, employing it in the
sense, not only of ecstatic excitement, but also of nothingness (5: 13). Isaiah, following the precedent of Micaiah,
goes so far as to assert that by means of ecstatic *Schwär-
merei* the Lord is misleading the prophets and the people
who blindly trust in them: they are imprisoned in un-
reality and enslaved by spiritual deadness (29: 13 ff.).

It is understandable, therefore, that the canonical
prophets stand over in sharpest contrast against the background furnished by the official prophesying of their
time. It is clearly part of their commission and vocation
to illuminate the true spiritual character of the latter. On
the other hand, the Biblical record implies that prophecy
is an institution of divine origin and character. The utter
falsehood into which contemporary prophesying has
sunk represents the degeneration of something noble and
spiritual in itself. The paradox of the situation resides in
the fact that the great prophets, while denouncing their
professional *confrères*, feel bound to characterize their
own inspired activity as prophesying. Amos, in the same

breath in which he declares that he is no *nabi*, also explains that the Lord had called him to prophesy: "Go prophesy [*hinnabe*] unto my people Israel" (7: 15). Especially revealing is Amos 3: 7, 8, which implies that there is an order of prophets to whom the divine counsels are esoterically revealed. The whole *raison d'être* of Amos' prophesying is that he belongs to this order and is impelled by the urge of the spirit to declare that which has been revealed to him in secret. Moreover, in certain passages, Yahwe is shown as remonstrating with His people on the ground that they have repudiated the regular succession of prophets whom He had raised up for their spiritual enlightenment. Jeremiah, in a recurrent vividly anthropomorphic phrase, represents this divine calling of the prophets as a proof of the ever-active providence of God: "I sent unto them My servants the prophets, rising up early and sending them; but ye would not hear, saith the Lord" (29: 19); cf. 35: 15. Similarly, in Amos, Yahwe, in expostulating with His wayward children, points out that He has unfailingly raised up prophets: "And I raised up of your sons for prophets and of your young men for Nazirites" (Amos 2: 11). In Deuteronomy, the prophetic office is credited with divine authority. It is Israel's distinctive possession, differentiating her from the surrounding peoples who practise augury and divination. "I will raise them up a prophet from among their brethren, like unto thee; and I will put My words in his mouth and he shall speak unto them all that I shall command him" (Deut. 18: 18). We have to consider whether the canonical prophets are to be classed among these *nebiim* who seem to have enjoyed an official and a divinely sanctioned status in the community. This issue is one of immediate interest, owing to the challenging and clear-cut hypothesis thrown out by Jepsen, who declares that there is an absolute solution of continuity between the official *nebiim* and the great writing prophets. The latter, with the exception of Haggai and Zechariah and possibly Nahum and Habbakuk, do not belong to the history of

Nebiismus and do not style themselves *nabi*.[1] It is true that the vocation of Jeremiah is designated as that of "prophet unto the nations", but Jepsen explains that the term *nabi* is here used in the quite general sense of *Sprecher Gottes* (spokesman of God) and not in its specialized meaning as denoting the member of a particular profession.[2] Again, when the contemporaries of Ezekiel are told that they should recognize the presence of a prophet in their midst, the word *nabi* is used in its general and not in its particular sense.[3] Other passages implying that the canonical prophets are technical *nebiim* are eliminated on grounds of textual criticism. For example, the highly important passages already quoted from Amos are eliminated on the consideration that they spring from a *nebiistische Überarbeitung* of the book, from a "revision in the interests of the *nebiim*".[4]

According to Jepsen, the sharp distinction between the writing prophet and the *nabi* arises from the fact that the latter is a psychic and charismatically endowed personality.[5] The ideal *nabi* is filled with the Spirit in the power of which he is able to perform miracles and mighty deeds. It is felt that the *nebiim* are in the secure and abiding possession of prophetic talents which confer upon them a certain measure of independence over against the God who is the ultimate source of those talents. The spiritual endowment of the *nabi* operates as a current of psychic energy which impregnates, for example, an Elijah's mantle or an Elisha's staff. The wonderful life-giving virtue of this spiritual power inheres even in the dead bones of the prophet (2 Kings 13: 21). The self-consciousness of the *nabi* is such that his impressive personality comes into the foreground of the picture, and a whole saga of legendary material is woven to glorify it. In contrast to the *nabi's* professionalism and reliance upon technical means of inspiration, the writing prophet is a man whose human personality counts for nothing in and for itself. He does not lay

---

[1] *op. cit.*, pp. 132–142   [2] *op. cit.*, p. 141   [3] *op. cit.*, p. 141
[4] *op. cit.*, p. 134   [5] *op. cit.*, p. 189

claim to spirit-possession and the visionary experience which it mediates. He does not perform deeds of power. Amos and Hosea are merely reeds to the divine voice— *personæ* in the literal sense of the term. The decisive characteristic of the writing prophet in northern Israel is constituted by the fact that his experience of God is unconditioned. It is God who acts and God who is glorified. Yahwe demands the unconditional surrender alike of prophet and of people. The new note is seen in the emphasis upon the sovereign freedom of God, who is not, as is implied in the outlook of the charismatic *nabi*, irretrievably linked to the destiny of Israel.[1]

These characteristic features of the consciousness of the writing prophets are emphasized and amplified in the section dealing with the history of *Nabitum* in Judah.[2] The *nabi* is a member of a certain profession, and, as such, he has mastered his technique, which he can use at will. The inspiration of the writing prophet, on the other hand, is uncontrollable and irresistible. The Word which he declares is an event which conquers him against his will, subduing his personality by the mysterious compelling power of divine Grace. It is not comprehensible by rational inference, it is not accessible to the grasp of human reason at all: it is the irrational and incalculable work of God breaking forth upon human personality with absolute demand.[3]

While this sharp contrast between the charismatic *nabi* and the writing prophet is eminently valuable and suggestive, it is possible to show that Jepsen has exaggerated it and that it is unjustifiable to deny all connexion between the two types. So far from the sense of divine compulsion creating an impassable gulf between the writing prophets and their predecessors, it is just that sense of divine compulsion which we see already manifested in the *nebiim* of the early period. It is significant that the note of otherness and driving constraint is the outstanding characteristic of the consciousness of Balaam —a heathen diviner. No more convincing example could

[1] Jepsen, *op. cit.*, pp. 189, 190   [2] *op. cit.*, pp. 191–217   [3] *op. cit.*, p. 215

be cited of what has been termed *Überwaltigung*—the domination of the prophet by his God. Balaam has every material incentive to prophesy the exact opposite of that which he does prophesy. But by an inner divine necessity he is compelled to disappoint the hopes of Balaak and to bless those whom he has been employed to curse. It is exactly the same kind of situation as that which arises (though with far greater poignancy) when a Jeremiah is constrained to announce tidings of woe and doom to the countrymen with whom he feels himself identified and whom he would fain see in prosperity. Even the purely ecstatic manifestations of a Saul come to him unexpectedly from a source outside himself. He does not seek these unusual experiences; rather, he employs a David in order to be released from their obsession. The same sense of compulsion by an irresistible power *ab extra* is the notable feature of the curious story in 1 Kings 13, where the prophet is suddenly compelled, at table, to contradict the lie with which he had persuaded the man of God to accept his hospitality. Micaiah at first—probably out of regard to conformity and politeness—joins his voice to the chorus of false prophets who predict success. But when pressed to reveal the truth in the name of the Lord, he cannot maintain the artifice: he must declare what he has seen and heard. Always there is this element of inevitability about true prophecy, whether it belongs to the early or the classical period.

Secondly, Jepsen appears to build too much upon the fact that the canonical prophets fail to base their experience of the Word upon spirit-possession. Whereas, for the *nabi*, the capacity to receive and declare the divine Word is grounded in the prior possession of the Spirit, no such limiting condition attaches to the experience of the canonical prophets who "appeal only to Yahweh's Word".[1] Since Jepsen regards the spirit-possession of the *nabi* as a kind of professional mantic technique, the distinction which he thus establishes is that between the psychic adept and the humble layman through whom

[1] *op. cit.*, p. 215

God speaks. Surely, however, it is wrong to regard the charismatic endowment of the *nabi* as a professional manticism which the prophet can manipulate at will. The essential characteristic of the theology of the *ruach* is that the invasion of the personality by the divine is a supernatural happening which lies utterly beyond human control. The *nabi* is as completely dependent upon inspiration as is the writing prophet. So far as the psychological structure of their experience is concerned, no radical distinction can rightly be drawn between them. The only difference is that, in the case of the *nabi*, we have an explicit psychological theory in terms of which the experience of inspiration is interpreted. But this theory is equally applicable to the experience of the writing prophet, which is psychologically continuous with that of the *nabi*.

Indeed, the real and valid distinction between *nabi* and writing prophet cannot be grounded in psychological considerations at all, since psychology concerns only the external form of consciousness. It is not determinative of its inner quality and content. This external form varies with historical circumstance and individual temperament. Jepsen says that the writing prophets have no visions[1] and he regards this psychological factor as decisive for the characterization of their consciousness. Even if the truth of this contention were quite indisputable, it would not necessarily indicate a qualitative differentiation between them and their predecessors. It is true, as we have seen, that nearly all the visions of the writing prophets revolve around the kernel of normal sense-impressions, whereas in such a figure as that of Elisha we seem to detect a psychic predisposition for second sight and hearing which play a predominantly large part in his consciousness. The same psychic predisposition reappears, however, in the person of Ezekiel, whose visual hallucinations are unusually keen. But this abnormal element in his experience in no way diminishes the original quality of his message.

[1] *op. cit.*, p. 215

Again, the canonical prophets do not inveigh against the false prophets because these latter have an ecstatic spirit-possessed consciousness, but because their visionary ecstasy is an empty and delusive form without vital significance and genuine spiritual justification. The presupposition of their polemic is that the *ruach* by which the *nebiim* claim to be possessed should be the mediator of revealed truth. It is this generally accepted belief which makes the pretensions of the *nebiim* all the more criminal, and it is the palpable contradiction between their spiritual claims and the falsehood of their message which forms the object of attack. The false prophets are degrading and exploiting spiritual inspiration for their own selfish ends. But they can only simulate its forms: they do not know its power and reality. Thus, Micah, in the passages in which he so vehemently attacks the false prophets, makes it clear that he has a personal vision and realization of the true character of the Spirit (2: 7; 3: 8). The polemic in Ezekiel and Jeremiah is not to be understood as a denunciation of spirit-possession as such, but only as an attack upon its artificial fabrication by a class of persons who have ceased to experience its living power. Vision, dream, ecstasy—the dead structure of religious experience remains when the vitalizing Spirit which filled it has fled. Ezek. 13: 3 expressly states that it is their own spirit which the false prophets follow, in contradistinction to the Spirit of the Lord which should come upon them *ab extra*, bending and subduing them to its own purposes. It would be equally erroneous to suppose that the Isaianic reference to the spirit of deep sleep (Isa. 29: 10) is an allusion to real spirit-possession. Here, Isaiah is making use of the current *ruach*-formula to account for a phenomenon so extraordinary as to be unexplainable on a rational hypothesis. It is simply the characteristically Hebrew way of saying that the spiritual dullness and obtuseness of the prophets is so marked as to pass the bounds of the normal and the natural.

Thus, spirit-possession is not always, as Jepsen implies, a false *Rausch* which the canonical prophets object to on grounds of principle. In fact, there is nothing to indicate that the false prophets were more ecstatic than the true. If, as we shall hope to show, the source of their prophecies is rational inference and calculation as opposed to genuine inspiration, it is possible that, in the later stages of the prophetic movement, they were less subject to ecstasy than the writing prophets. The false prophets are obsessed by a fixed rationalistic theology and they simulate ecstatic experience in order to give it a show of justification. Their dreams and visions are lying vanities just because they are sterile forms and not a creative source of inspiration. So far from being its antithesis, spirit-possession, as we have contended in a previous chapter, is the natural psychological framework into which the consciousness of the great prophets is most easily fitted. The invasion of the human personality by the divine *ruach* is a translation into the terms of Hebrew psychology of that immediate and unconditioned experience of God which Jepsen predicates of the canonical prophets.

In the blossoming of the prophetic consciousness of Amos and his successors, we see the highest peak attained by the charismatic movement of *Nabitum*. Of this movement, the false prophets of Jeremiah's time are degenerate survivors, aping blindly dead forms inherited from the past. The difference between the canonical prophets and their predecessors, the sons of the prophets, is best explained in biological rather than in psychological terms. It is not a difference of radical opposition between antithetic psychological forms (as is implied in the theory that the canonical prophets repudiated all experience of the Spirit), but rather a distinction between higher and lower types of consciousness. Perhaps this difference may be best explained in terms of the analogy furnished by the conception of emergent evolution. The higher consciousness of the canonical prophet arises out of the lower consciousness of the *nabi* by a seemingly natural process of development. Yet the higher could not have been predicted from, nor can it be accounted for on the basis of, the lower. It represents a spiritualization and deepening of the latter, so that the psychological structure of the experience is now seen as incidental rather than essential. In the case of the *nabi*, attention is focused on the psychological form which his experience takes. He strikes his contemporaries as a madman—*meshuga'*, משנע (Hos. 9: 7; 2 Kings 9: 11). But, with the writing prophet, this psychological form becomes the vehicle of a spiritual insight which expresses the quality of his personality. It is filled with a content of revolutionary power and significance. This distinction was not realized by the average onlooker who was ill-qualified to appreciate the originality and depth of the prophetic message. No outward sign, appreciable by all, distinguished the two classes of men. This is proof that the writing prophets belonged integrally to the *nabi* movement. The psychological accompaniments of their inspired state were such that men found it natural to identify them with the lower type. Hence the curious fact that, despite their anxiety to dissociate themselves from the official *nebiim*, no word but *hithnabbe* can be found to designate the special activity to which they have been divinely commissioned. The very manner of their speech stamps them as "ecstatics". Amaziah, the high priest, in dismissing Amos from the sanctuary at Bethel appears to have referred to his prophesying by the term נמף (*nataph*). The use of this verb indicates that the prophetic word was conceived as a stream which gushes forth. Sometimes it was accompanied by loud cries and excited gestures. Ezekiel is told to cry and howl (21: 11); to smite upon his thigh (21: 11) and stamp with his foot (6: 11). In the prophetic books we have no smooth, reasoned didactic exposition, resting upon the logical processes of thought, but a collection of spontaneous poetic utterances poured forth in the heat of the Spirit, in moments of heightened consciousness. The germ of the prophetic oracles lies in some God-given impulse, some spark of inspiration struck from the heart of those familiar sights and sounds which surround the prophet

in daily life. It may be some spectacle in which the Spirit
leads him to behold a sign, or some remark, uttered
casually, yet to the prophetic ear pregnant with hidden
suggestiveness. But, whatever the immediate occasion,
the inspired oracle forms itself upon the prophet's lips
swiftly, unexpectedly, impulsively. It is the antithesis of
reflective thought.

We see, then, that there is no radical opposition
between the writing prophet and the charismatic *nabi*.
We can only place the former in his true historical perspective, and understand his psychology aright, if we see
him as the fine flower of the *nabi* movement. He transcends that out of which he has grown so that the psychological factors, which seemed to be central and determinative in prophetic experience, are now pushed to the
circumference to make room for the emergence of a
consciousness which belongs to an infinitely higher level
of spiritual development. Those factors are now relegated
to the status of peripheral accompaniments whose inci-
dence depends upon personal and historical circumstance. Thus, there is a violent recrudescence of psychic
abnormality in Ezekiel, whose mediumistic personality
lends itself to the production of such phenomena.

If, however, there is no such radical opposition
between the two types as Jepsen postulates, how are we
to explain the bitterness of the conflict with the official
nebiim in which the writing prophets find themselves
engaged? How shall we account for their anxiety to
repudiate all connexion with the official representatives
of prophecy? In order to answer these questions, we have
to turn our attention to the existence and character of
yet a third class of prophets who are essentially alien to
the sharply characterized culture and psychology of
Israel. These are the ecstatic priest-prophets, attached to
the sanctuaries of the ancient near East. We can only
begin to divine the vital significance of the *nabi* movement which culminates in great prophets of the Bible,
when we set it against the background of the professional
priest-prophet. The professional priest-prophet is the

master of a technique which enables him to cultivate ecstasy at will. He may have been marked out for his vocation by the possession of psychic gifts, but the important point is that, for him, the giving of oracles in ecstasy is a craft into whose secrets he has been initiated by training. Such priest-prophets usually worked in bands, since the ecstasy which they cultivated could be attained more easily by gregarious activity. The Bible presents us with two scenes in which the functions and the behaviour of such prophets are vividly depicted— the Baal-prophets on Mount Carmel and the court prophets of Ahab in 1 Kings 22. The Baal prophets may be regarded as the representatives of the Canaanite ritualistic system; they are competing with the Mosaic champion Elijah for the allegiance of Israel. They belong to the personnel of the Canaanite sanctuaries; and the Mount Carmel episode is of the most vital significance, for it shows how, alongside of the adoption of the Canaanite myth and ritual pattern, went the adoption of the Canaanite method of prophecy. These priest-prophets are experts in the art of transporting themselves at will into an ecstatic frenzy in order to become "god-possessed". They shout in chorus a monotonous cry. They use magic, whether it be that of the sacred dance or of symbolic action. Perhaps also they employed sexual and alcoholic indulgence. The final result is that in this passionate yearning and expansion of their being, they feel that they have become god, that god is in them and they in god.

Now there is a clear and definite distinction between this deliberately induced ecstasy and the psychology of the *nabi* movement. The beginnings of the latter are shrouded in obscurity, but it seems that at first the *nabi* underwent the infection of Canaanite ecstasy. This is suggested by the fact that the band of prophets whom Saul meets have come down from the sanctuary on the hill of God and that their ecstatic prophesying appears to have been stimulated by liturgical music. Even Elisha calls for music in order to awaken his prophetic

inspiration (2 Kings 3: 15). But, despite this, it is clear
that the *nebiim* of Israel soon differentiated themselves in a
decisive manner from the priest-prophet of the sanctuaries. They were independent and at first had no
recognized and official status in the community. Despised by those of settled rank, they roamed wildly about
the countryside, at least in northern Israel. They were
openly regarded as fools and madmen (2 Kings 9: 11)
and were mischievously mocked by children. They bore
the badge of the proletariat, so that men found it natural
to ask: Who is their father? (1 Sam. 10: 12). Astonish-
ment was general when Saul, the son of a well-established
and prosperous farmer, joined their ranks. Nevertheless,
their psychic endowment compelled a certain super-
stitious veneration. They were "men of God", imbued
with mana, and signal punishment overtook those who
offended them.

But, from our present point of view, their most
important feature was that they were nationalists and
Yahwe enthusiasts, strenuously opposed to the infiltra-
tion of the Canaanite religious system. They stand in a
special relationship of trust in, and absolute dependence
on, Yahwe. They are urged by the conviction of a
mission which they have to fulfil. Called by Yahwe, they
are endowed by Him with the spiritual equipment for
their office. They are pre-eminently men of the Spirit.
They have no technique, they do not voluntarily adopt
the office of prophet. They are driven wherever the Spirit
leads. When the Spirit comes upon them, they cannot but
yield and obey this obstinate inward urge. Elisha spontaneously abandons his agricultural labour, and cuts the
ties that bind him to his home (1 Kings 19: 19 ff.). Their
entire prophetic activity is determined by the Word and
Spirit of Yahwe in whose power they stand. They
interpret their experience in terms of their native Hebrew
psychology. Their theology of the *ruach* emphasizes the
priority of God and man's dependence upon Him.
Nothing that they could do would be of any avail to
compel the presence of the Spirit. Technical means could

but produce the psychological condition of ecstatic rapture, which is a very different thing from possession by the Spirit of the Lord. Elisha desires and petitions ardently a double portion of Elijah's spirit, but he cannot merit or force the gift. These *nebiim* of northern Israel are as utterly dependent upon God as the Psalmist who cried: "Take not Thy Holy Spirit from me." They are the true prototype of the canonical prophet, and stand in sharpest contrast to the heathen priest-prophet of the sanctuaries. They are independent of both courtly and priestly influences.

The case is somewhat different with the *nebiim* of Judah who are raised to an official status at David's court, which is shaped by Canaanite influences. On the model of the Canaanite religious system, an alliance is established between priest and *nabi*.[1] Nathan and Zadok, together with Benaiah, the commander of the standing army, form the progressive party at the royal court and perhaps connive at some form of compromise with Canaanite culture.[2] This Canaanitish alliance between priest and prophet becomes thenceforth decisive for the future development of prophecy in Judah. Here the *nebiim*, in contrast to the position which they held in northern Israel, belong to the upper classes of the community. They are wealthy and prone to succumb to the temptation of avarice. Constantly, in the Judean prophets, we find that priest and prophet are coupled together as leaders of the people who have been false to their trust.[3] Moreover, these *nebiim* of Judah are dependent upon the royal court for their emoluments and official status,[4] hence all too readily they yield to the temptation of trying to secure their position by prophesying in accordance with the wishes and declared policy of the King. They think too that their possession of the Spirit is governed by their enjoyment of an assured official position.[5] Zedekiah's self-confidence is grounded in the belief that since he possesses the royal favour and

---

[1] Jepsen, *op. cit.*, p. 154   [2] *op. cit.*, p. 155   [3] e.g. Mic. 3: 11; Jer. 5: 31; etc.
[4] Jepsen, *op. cit.*, p. 193   [5] *op. cit.*, p. 199

an established status, his prophetic counsel must be authentic. The Spirit of Yahwe cannot have departed from him to rest upon an obscure and unofficial prophet such as Micaiah. There is an obvious parallel between this attitude and that of the professional priest-prophet who relies upon his accredited position at the sanctuary and his knowledge of his craft.

In course of time it seems that the official court prophets, who exercised their profession in the temple at Jerusalem, lost that spiritual vigour, integrity and forth-rightness which was so characteristic of Nathan, and became corrupted both by their gradual approximation to the Canaanitish priest-prophets and by the fact that they were so firmly embedded in the sociological struc-ture of the State. It is probable that they adopted and assiduously practised the mantic technique in use among the heathen priest-prophets, while making it a means of buttressing their preconceptions, and the orthodox views and policy of the royal court.

It is certainly against these official *nebiim* of Judah, whose prophesying was modelled on the Canaanite ritualistic pattern, that the polemic of the canonical pro-phets is launched. It could not have been in the spiritual and enthusiastic *nebiim* of northern Israel that they dis-covered targets for their scorn and mockery. For, as we have seen, the latter formed the very type out of which the writing prophets emerged, and they held all foreign influences in abhorrence. But in the official priest-prophets of Jerusalem the writing prophets saw the exact antithesis of all that they themselves stood for. It is noticeable that the controversy with false prophets is mainly the concern of Micah, Isaiah, Jeremiah and Ezekiel, whose prophecies were directed to the people of Judah. This polemic reveals that those against whom they inveigh are men who, by imbibing the culture of a foreign civilization, have betrayed the original creative spirit of the religion of Israel. The burden of Isaiah's invective is that these priest-prophets are drunk—no doubt a reference to the use of intoxicants as a means of exciting ecstatic inspiration (28: 7). According to Jeremiah, the dream is one of the predominant forms of their inspiration (23: 25), while in one passage he implies that the people's obstinate self-deception was encouraged by a host of diviners, soothsayers and sorcerers (27: 9). The polemic of Ezekiel reveals the existence of a class of prophetesses who, like the heathen *shamans*, had power over the souls of men, driving them from the body and pursuing and injuring them (13: 17ff.).

But the deepest distinction between the canonical prophets and the false prophets has little to do with the outward forms of manticism. The former made ample use of such technical *procédés* as were common coin in the cultures of the ancient Near East—ecstatic vision and dream, Semitic divination and symbolic action. This ancient technique, however, is transformed in character and meaning by being made the vehicle of the Hebrew religious genius. The point is most clearly illustrated by the Hebrew reaction to the wave of ecstatic enthusiasm which swept over Palestine at the time of the Hebrew settlement there. That which had been merely the technique of attaining a certain psychological state becomes, in the Hebrew religious consciousness, a direct personal experience of God—reached not by training and professionalism, but by the unsought transformation of the personality under the impact of the divine energy. The use of symbolical action is common both to the writing prophets and their opponents, but, with the former, it is a means of promoting the divine purpose, whereas, with the latter, it represents a vain attempt to support and actualize the deceitful fancies of the heart.

Mantic technique is therefore a mere form whose value depends upon the content which fills it and the ends to which it is used. In his controversy with the false prophets of his time, we see Jeremiah gradually becoming aware of this fact.[1] The professional priest-prophets to whom

[1] In a rudimentary fashion, the problem was present to the minds of the authors of the Deuteronomic legislation who established two tests for the genuineness of prophecy: (1) its general moral and spiritual effect on the life of the people (Deut. 13); (2) its verification by the event (Deut. 18)

he is opposed are able to bring forth visions and dreams in abundance in attestation of their message. At first, Jeremiah allows himself to be impressed by the display of professional manticism which his opponents put forward, and he seems to take the mere condition of ecstasy as an indication that a genuine message has been received. He is evidently bewildered and embarrassed by the enthusiastic conviction of a Hananiah whom he has at first no means of refuting. In default of other criteria, he is compelled to leave the verification of his prophecy to the arbitrament of events. It seems that he has to await the coming of a new ecstatic inspiration of his own before he is able to return to Hananiah a reply which is backed by divine authority and can be truly described as a "word of the Lord".

Jeremiah's ultimate conclusion is suggested in the important section of his work, headed, "Concerning the prophets". Here there is no nice evaluation of the relative merits of various forms of prophecy, though certain expressions may be interpreted to mean that he ranks the audition as superior in spiritual value to the dream (23: 28). But the fundamental thesis of the chapter goes much deeper than any such survey. The prophet recognizes that the form through which the message is mediated constitutes no sure criterion of the character of its contents. The audition—the use of the formula "He saith"—may be just as spurious as the vision and dream (23: 31). That which stamps the false prophets as false is not the mere fact that they are adepts in the use of the professional manticism of their time, but that they lack the central and essential elements in the consciousness of the true prophet, viz., moral and spiritual fellowship with God, the genuine hearing of God's words and an authentic commission to speak in His name. The false prophets are they whose dreams and ecstasies are vitiated by their disastrous effect upon the moral life of the people. The test of the genuineness of prophetic inspiration lies in the spiritual fruits that it produces. Jeremiah has now learnt to distinguish form from content, and to realize that ecstasy, so far from guaranteeing the authenticity of a given prophecy, does but lend expression to the inner spiritual worth of the prophet's personality. The true prophet is he who has "stood in the council of Yahwe" (23: 18, 22) and "heard the word of Yahwe" (23: 18, 21, 28; 14: 14)—phrases which surely denote something far more fundamental and vital than any mystico-ecstatic audition. Such phrases suggest the incommunicable and unanalysable experience of all religious assurance. They imply that profound and confident insight into the secret thoughts and purposes of God which is the very essence of the consciousness of the great prophets. They indicate something spiritual and intrinsic rather than formal and technical. This is made clear from the record that we have of Jeremiah's own heart-searching inquiry into the ultimate grounds of his religious confidence. He reaches the conclusion that before he can become the mouthpiece of God he is called upon to sift and test the agitating suggestions which surge up in moments of ecstatic experience. He must make a creative value-judgment which will necessarily reflect the spiritual quality of his whole personality. Further, the prophetic consciousness, thrust upon him from the outside, can be sustained and developed only by the progressive spiritual purification of his inner life. The prophetic impulse was weakened in him in consequence of the tumult of warring feelings—vindictive desire, regret, dismay—which tossed in his soul. The experience of Jeremiah shows to what an extent the prophet's inspired insight depends upon the moral purity and elevation of his personal life.

We see therefore that the great Biblical prophets cannot dispense with the necessity for making a personal venture of faith, and it is just in this respect that they most decisively differentiate themselves from the professional priest-prophets to whom they were opposed. The former have no external and formal guarantee of the truth of their message; no experience, however striking and unusual, can vouch for its validity. It must stand or

fall by its intrinsic authority. That authority is inward
and spiritual and must be spiritually discerned. The
religious certainty of these prophets is rooted in their
personal spiritual consciousness of being in direct contact
with the living God. The professional prophets, on the
other hand, show no trace of this spiritual inwardness.
The ground of their assurance is external, formal and
technical. They believe themselves to be automatically
possessed of the Spirit in virtue of the official status which
they hold as the authoritative exponents of the will of
Yahwe. They are officially instituted as leaders of the
people and guardians of the faith and of public morality.
Doubtless, too, they came to rely more and more upon
the quasi-magical virtue and efficacy of the forms of
manticism which were predominant in the world of the
Canaanitish ritual culture. In their hands, the infectious
spiritual enthusiasm which characterized the early stages
of the *nabi* movement has become canalized and
petrified in certain specific media. The spiritual creative-
ness of Israel's religion has been lost in the course of this
process of progressive adaptation to the Canaanite
environment. Only some such hypothesis can explain the
instinctive repugnance and the passionate hostility which
the great prophets evince towards the technical official
prophets. The orthodox prophesying of their time is of
a piece with the immoral ritual system in which Yahwism
has become entangled and perverted. Hence, we see why
Amos was so keen to point out that he was a layman who
had his own secular avocation. *His call to prophesy, like
the call of each one of his successors, was an event in the world
of the spirit—an event determined by the Grace of God, and
independent of historical institutions.* The canonical prophets cannot even be said to have formed a class of
their own. Each is independent of the other, thrown
back upon the sheer directness of his peculiar personal
experience of God.

This deep distinction between the canonical prophet
and the priest-prophet generates an inevitable clash
between their respective theologies. The former stands

forth in fervent self-identification with the divine will
and judgment which he is spiritually authorized to
declare. The false prophet is the mouthpiece, not of the
wisdom of God, but of the temporal and self-centred
wisdom of the state. For him, the divine will is rationally
deducible from the accepted postulates of the current
theology. The honour of God is indissolubly linked to
the honour—the temporal destiny—of Israel. Man and
God are partners in a common end which is dictated by
mutual interests. This dream that God, for the sake of
His personal honour, must be on man's side was shattered by the first God-centred prophet to arise, viz.,
Amos; but was partially revived by Ezekiel in whom
(accepting the traditional view of the book) the pure
spirit of prophecy is adulterated by the prophet's evident
desire to come to terms with the national religion. The
quarrel between Jeremiah and the swarm of false prophets and politicians who opposed him turns wholly on
this issue. It is the spirit of conservative nationalism
which he arouses to implacable hatred. He looks out
upon the world from God's angle of vision and therefore
sees the loud and clamorous patriotism of his countrymen
for what it truly is—the blind obduracy and self-
centredness of man's heart which refuses to submit to
the judgment of God. But, for the common type of *nabi*,
the governing purpose and activity of Yahwe were
essentially accessible and comprehensible to the human
reason. They held fast to a theodicy which is reflected in
the books of Nahum and Habbakuk and which inevitably comes into conflict with the irrational aspect of
reality. They committed the ever-recurrent error of
making man the measure of God. The annihilating Word
of judgment sounded false in their ears. Their prophecy
consisted in the inferential calculation of events on the
basis of their theological presuppositions.

In opposition to this rational theodicy, the canonical
prophets based their prophecies upon the intuitions
which sprang from their immediate and incommunicable
consciousness of standing in the presence of God. The

God with whom they had to do was the hidden God, the secrets of whose sway were unfathomable by the logic of human discourse. Unredeemed, natural man is blind and deaf and insensible to the mysterious workings of the divine Spirit. Israel's heart was hardened equally against Amos' declaration of the nation's imminent destruction and against Isaiah's declaration that, for the faithful, the holy city would be miraculously preserved. Yahwe, by the unpredictable incalculable movements of His Grace, overthrows all human inferences, however sagacious; all rational schemes, however neatly devised. Accepting the assumptions of the current rationalistic theodicy, it would have been impossible to suppose that Yahwe, as a punishment for sin, could actually *destroy* the people to whom by the necessities of His own existence He seemed irretrievably committed. Likewise, Isaiah's insistence upon the adequacy and efficacy of faith alone seemed utterly contrary to reason in face of the military situation of the time.

The refreshing originality and daring of these utterances is vitally connected with the freedom and independence of the writing prophet's position *vis-à-vis* the State. Unlike the cult prophet, he does not feel bound, by professional ties, to support the existing order of things. He preserves inviolate his inner freedom: no conflict of loyalties hinders him from giving expression to that which the Spirit dictates. The court prophet and the priest-prophet, on the contrary, had a natural interest in the preservation of the sociological structure in which they had secured their permanent niche. Self-interest blinded them to the inner corruption which irrevocably sealed its final doom. Their uncritical acceptance of the received eschatology fortified them in this complacent outlook. Hence arises that secret, deep depravity which warps their moral vision and leads them to call good evil and evil good. They wish to reduce and schematize the mighty working of God in accordance with the requirements of their own faithless desires.

Chapter Four

THE RELIGIOUS PSYCHOLOGY OF THE HEBREW PROPHETIC CONSCIOUSNESS

ONE of the main problems which arise in any study of the psychology of the prophetic consciousness is that of the importance which we are to attach to the abnormal or ecstatic element in their experience. We have shown in the previous chapter that the great prophets are distinguished from their predecessors by the emergence in them of a new spiritual quality of consciousness which presents us with a phenomenon *sui generis*. We have still, however, to draw out the general psychological implications of the prophetic consciousness considered as an *état d'esprit*.

In discussing prophetic psychology, it is of the utmost importance to define the precise shade of meaning which we are to attach to the much-abused term "ecstasy". *Prima facie*, this term is not a very appropriate one to use in connexion with the psychology of the Hebrews, for it presupposes the Greek view of man as an incarnate soul. In Greek psychology, ecstasy is a state in which the soul temporarily leaves its fleshly prison-house, and journeys forth unhindered by fleshly limitations.[1] With a more general reference to Western psychology, ecstasy denotes loss of consciousness consequent upon extreme mental concentration. But the term is used widely to denote all uplifted states of mind. In its more general use, it indicates a unification and enhancement of consciousness, in which there is an intense emotional realization of the ultimate value and significance of that which absorbs the attention. In such a state, the being is simplified and concentrated. All its psychic energies are gathered up into one full flowing tide, with the result that the object upon which the mind devotedly gazes is made vividly

[1] Hölscher, *op. cit.*, p. 1

present to consciousness. In ecstasy, there is no enlargement of the range of conceptual knowledge, but there is a peculiarly vivid sense of knowing. That which a man has hitherto known only theoretically now becomes living and palpable.

It is unfortunate that, in the controversy which has raged around the question whether the Biblical prophets are to be regarded as ecstatics, attention has been concentrated upon the abnormal psycho-physical effects of ecstasy and no attempt has been made to elucidate the psychology of the prophetic consciousness on its more normal and balanced side. Thus, Hölscher, who contends that the great prophets are to be interpreted as ecstatic in this extreme sense, draws a picture in which the prophet emerges as a psychopathic case; and, in order to support his contention, has to make excessive and frequent reference to small scraps of evidence culled from apocalyptic and New Testament sources, as well as from the prophets themselves. Ecstasy is described as a kind of oscillation between violent emotional exaltation and nervous exhaustion.[1] In its "sthenic" form it is marked by excited movements of the hands and feet, such as we find in Ezekiel; loud, almost involuntary cries, such as are characteristic of the prophetic speech of Jeremiah; and inevitably it gives birth to song and dance.[2] Physically, it produces such effects as muscular tension, acceleration of the heart, breath, and pulse, and an expansion of the peripheral vessels which become flooded with blood.[3] Apathetic ecstasy is associated with anxiety and fear, and follows overwhelming visionary experience.[4] Its effects are paralysing, as is seen in St. Paul's blindness and Ezekiel's dumbness. In the abnormal psychological state provoked by ecstasy, an important change takes place in the mode of the mind's operation. The manifold succession of thoughts is arrested and the mind is frozen by the cramping tyranny of an *idée fixe*.[5] The ecstatic becomes the helpless

[1] *op. cit.*, pp. 4 ff.   [2] *op. cit.*, p. 7   [3] *op. cit.*, p. 5
[4] *op. cit.*, p. 13   [5] *op. cit.*, p. 16

plaything of psychic forces which assail his consciousness: his exhausted apperception is surrendered to whatever associations confront it. His movements are thenceforth impulsive, proceeding from the obsession which holds the consciousness in its grip.

Such a mental state is essentially one of disintegration. The normal composure of the mind is dissolved before the onset of an emotional storm with which it is unable to deal successfully. "The stronger the emotion, the more disorganized is the experience as a whole."[1] The mind becomes the victim of hallucinations and illusions: it loses its powers of perception and judgment: its correspondence with objective reality, on which sanity depends, is broken. Such is the psychological condition denoted by the reflexive verb *hithnabbe*. Delirium is the very hall-mark of ecstasy: "This condition of madness is really characteristic of the ecstatic prophet."[2] The symbolic acts of the prophets are, in Hölscher's view, purely impulsive actions—*Triebhandlungen*—determined by this abnormal psychic state.[3] The idea which obsesses the consciousness tends automatically to realize itself in outward action, since it is not opposed by other associations and the control of the will is impaired. The sense of compulsion which we have seen to be so important a characteristic of the prophetic consciousness is interpreted as a quasi-physical coercion arising from the loss of control over the play of the muscles. Thus, ecstasy is confused with glossolaly.[4]

These views are extremely debatable and spring from a false and one-sided conception of ecstatic experience. Whereas we should argue that ecstasy involves a unification and enhancement of consciousness producing vivid realization, Hölscher defines ecstasy as a state of mind involving disintegration and loss of balance. Secondly, he considers that ecstatic delirium provides a favourable disposition for, if it is not indeed the source of, visions

[1] *op. cit.*, p. 20. *Je stärker der Affekt ist, um so ungegliederter ist das Gesamterlebnis*

[2] *op. cit.*, p. 20. *Dieser Zustand des Rasens ist für den ekstatischen Profeten der eigentlich Kennzeichnende*

[3] *op. cit.*, pp. 30, 31

[4] *op. cit.*, pp. 31–35

and hallucinations.[1] But we consider that the visionary experience of the prophets reposes upon quite a different set of presuppositions. Not *starke Gefühle und Affekte*, but the methods of the Semitic diviner, the special psychology of the Semite and the operation of a dramatic and visual imagination, are the most important factors to be taken into account in any explanation of their visionary hallucinations. Thirdly, Hölscher is surely wrong in supposing that the symbolic actions of the prophets are purely impulsive. In point of fact, they are to be assigned to causes wholly other than psychic abnormality. They are rooted in the naïve realism of the Semitic *Weltanschauung*: they are performed with an earnestness and deliberation, a rational lucidity, an intense creative faith, which are far removed from the impulsive half-conscious conduct of the somnambulist and hypnotic.

Hölscher's definition of ecstasy does not enable us to characterize truly the essential features of the prophetic consciousness. The psychopathic condition which ecstasy sometimes involves is accidental and relative. It arises in personalities whose threshold of consciousness is mobile, lending itself readily to mono-ideism. It furnishes no criterion of the quality and strength of creative inspiration. Any idea, good or bad, can provoke extreme ecstasy in a mind which tends to become easily entranced. Of all the prophets of the Old Testament, only Ezekiel can be properly described in terms of Hölscher's psychology of ecstasy. In his experience, we see poise and self-control lost in the psychic storms which sweep over his personality; his mind is congealed in the grip of an *idée fixe*; his faculties and physical organs are temporarily impaired; while, on recovering consciousness, he finds himself in a condition of complete nervous exhaustion. It is stated that after his first visionary experience he remained in a state of sheer stupor for seven days —an instance of "apathetic ecstasy", and of ligature or loss of muscular control. At other times, he seems to have experienced levitation; he was conscious of being lifted

[1] *op. cit.*, p. 21

up, whirled through space, dragged hither and thither
by some power external to himself and without his
voluntary concurrence. He was also subject to catalepsy
—the cold rigidity and corpse-like condition the body
assumes in trance states. This is probably the explanation of the divine command to lie in a fixed position for
a considerable period of time. The physical impediment
consequent upon his abnormal psychic experience is
seen retrospectively to be imbued with divine significance.

We see, therefore, that Hölscher's understanding of
ecstasy enables us to define merely that which lies on the
outer fringe of the prophetic consciousness: we have now
to investigate the psychology which underlies its central
zone. We shall attempt to elicit the psychological implications of that sense of religious certainty which is conveyed by the formula *Ko amar Yahwe*. The basic factor
of the experience which determines the use of this
formula is an inspired state of mind—the mechanism of
contemplation—which the prophet shares with all
persons of creative genius, artist, poet and mystic. To say
that the prophetic experience is one of complete ecstasy
—in the sense in which that term is used in the technical
language of mystical theology—would involve us in the
supposition that the prophetic words were uttered in the
unconsciousness of the trance-state—a theory of prophetic inspiration which is quite as mechanical and
artificial as that demanded by the doctrine of the infalli-
bility of Holy Scripture. If the oracles of the prophet
depended upon his becoming rapt in ecstatic trance, then
his human personality would contribute nothing to the
complex event of revelation which in our view is a unity
in duality springing from the mysterious moment of
contact between the divine and human spirits. Prophetic
inspiration means, not the absorption or dissolution of
the prophet's personality (which the ecstatic theory,
properly speaking, presupposes), but its unification and
enhancement in an intense act of exalted imaginative
perception or vision, which quite transcends the measure

of the everyday consciousness with its multiple interests and distractions, and in which the eye of the soul is opened to the reality of the transcendental world. We have already indicated that the term "ecstasy" may be used to denote this state of enhanced consciousness, and the justification for this usage lies in the fact that such a state springs from *recueillement*, or the concentration of attention—a concentration which, if carried to its farthest limit, issues in the unconsciousness of trance. We may agree that the prophets were ecstatics, if the term ecstasy is used to denote an uplifted state of mind, dominated by a current of inspiration which collects, unifies and simplifies the whole being. Here we have a state of the highest integration, for the attention is wholly focused upon a single object which gradually fills the consciousness until the connexion between the subject and the outside world is broken. The strenuous exertion of the will is replaced by a quiet passivity, and the processes of conceptual thought give way to an intense emotional awareness of value and the feeling of domination by that which is objectively given in the synthetic unity of experience. Hence arises the characteristic sense of compulsion and possession: the subject in ineffable bliss knows himself to be united in the interior depths of his being to the ultimately Real to which he is now completely surrendered. Important as are the differences which divide them, the prophet, the poet, and the mystic, are one in virtue of the fundamental identity of that mental mechanism which characterizes their creative attitudes and experiences: they are linked in essential kinship by their characteristic approach to reality, by the kind of knowledge which makes them what they are. In order to illuminate the psychology of the prophetic consciousness, it will be necessary to look a little closer at this mental mechanism.

At the peak point of mystical or intuitional activity, the normal faculties of knowing, proper to the rational man, are held in abeyance in order that they may be transcended by the direct, supernatural self-bestowal of the divine Spirit. Meister Eckhart declaims against memory, understanding and will, as being sources of distraction and obscuration to the mystical unification and illumination of the consciousness: the self-emptying of the mind appears to him as the ideal.[1] St. Theresa says: "When God elevates the soul to union with Himself, He suspends the natural activity of all its powers, in order the more effectively to infuse into it true wisdom. Hence it sees not, neither hears, nor understands, as long as it remains united to its God."[2] This suspension of the mental faculties which lie at the periphery of the soul, while the divine presence is imparted to the soul's deepest life, is the real meaning of that passivity which we have seen to be a dominant and essential feature of uplifted states of consciousness. That which takes place in this most intimate union of the divine and human spirits is not the enlargement of the domain of man's rational knowledge of God, but the approach of the living God Himself to the central zone of the soul, giving rise to the vivid and impregnable certainty of possessing and being possessed by the divine presence. We may not even speak of the soul's insight into a fresh range of divine truths, for, in this moment of rapt communion, no discovery of new truth is attained, but rather the vastly enhanced realization and appropriation of truth already known. Pratt concludes his discussion by affirming that what is new in the experience is not the newness of the truth perceived but the union of familiar ideas with vivid emotion.[3] Indeed, ideas which had lain in the outer layers of the mind and were realized only by the conceptual, analytic mode of knowledge, now reverberate through the depths of the personality and seem to embody themselves in concrete actuality so that the subject feels himself to be gripped by their otherness and objectivity. Inspiration does not enrich those who are poor in intellectual and spiritual endowment, nor does it effect any radical change in the degree of our enlightenment, but it

---

[1] Pratt, *The Religious Consciousness*, p. 414
[2] Quoted by H. Brémond in *Prière et Poésie*, p. 157   [3] *op. cit.*, p. 411

simplifies and illuminates the confused and distracted consciousness, giving it a tranquillity in which it realizes with a new assurance, and sense of discovery, those things which it truly possessed: in such a mood of internal light and peace the seeds obscurely germinating in the hidden depths of the unconscious are found to burst into flower as under the fostering influence of sunlight. Further, there exists the closest and most positive relation between these two ways of knowledge, between the experimental communion with the Real, characteristic of mystical states, and those rational faculties of will, imagination and intellect whose operation is thereby temporarily checked. For the passivity of the state, the suspension of these faculties, is more apparent than real. This seeming immobility is a cloak under which the most intense creative activity is being prepared. So soon as the rapture dies away, the faculties of the natural man are seen to renew themselves with immensely quickened life and vigour. They profit by the deepened emotional realization of truth, by the exultant and expansive contact of the soul with reality, and they reflect the dazzling radiation which now suffuses the inner being of the man. Now is the time when the creative artist feels himself carried along by the furious and ever-waxing momentum of his inspiration: the joyful sense of having been plunged into the heart of things means that his genius or talents operate with redoubled power and intensity. Thoughts and images surge at his bidding, and so compelling is his mood that he feels like one possessed, surrendered to the domination of some external force. Ample testimony to the sense of compulsion and possession experienced by creative artists and so strikingly parallel to the phenomena of the Hebrew prophetic consciousness, is collected by R. Harding in *Anatomy of Inspiration* (p. 13 ff.). Flaubert said: "*Mes personnages m'affectent, me poursuivent, ou plutôt c'est moi qui suis eux.*"[1]

We are now in a position to consider how the psychology of the intuitional consciousness illuminates the

[1] Quoted by Brémond, *op. cit.*, p. 151

experience veiled rather than expressed in the formula
Ko amar Yahwe. We have already suggested that it
would be far too literalistic and short-sighted to take this
formula at its face-value as necessarily implying the
audition of external spoken words. It would mean
making a facile and superficial assimilation—regardless
of historical probabilities—of the Hebrew prophetic consciousness to a very secondary, occasional, and comparatively unimportant aspect of Western mysticism. The
phrase expresses a far deeper and more fundamental
significance. It indicates a special variety of religious
experience—the variety constituted by that experimental
knowledge of God which we have been discussing, and
which flowers in a developed form, wherever religion,
rising above its primitive origins, flows from a transcendental revelation to elect spirits. What the prophet
wishes to express by his solemn declaration is the
creative, epoch-making encounter of his own soul with
the divine, his inspired assurance that the truths he
utters are not the production of his own mind but a
revelation from the heart of reality. In order to communicate his conviction of the sheer objectivity and
otherness of the truth which springs to birth in his mind,
he must perforce have resort to the only set of terms
which he feels to be appropriate—the symbolism (as we
should regard it) involved in supposing that his words are
identical with those of Yahwe. In prefacing his oracles
with the august phrase, the Hebrew prophet is saying in
his own peculiarly Hebrew way what the mystics and
inspired personalities of every race and civilization unite
in affirming, viz., that on the heights of their ineffable
experiences they are not communing with their own
souls, but are being sharply and tensely confronted by
the eternal Reality which transcends their consciousness
and beats upon it like the exhausing heat of the noonday
sun. We may suppose, therefore, that the experience
which authenticates and justifies the use of the formula
Ko amar Yahwe is precisely that experience of experimental communion with God, of creative inspiration, or

of mystical awareness—however we may wish to phrase it—which is the basic and vitalizing experience of all inspired persons, prophet, mystic, poet and artist.

But, in applying the psychology of the intuitional consciousness to the prophetic state of mind, one notable difficulty arises. It is that of relating the prophet's deep mystical awareness to the cognitive aspect of this consciousness. There is a sharp dissimilarity, as well as a fundamental kinship, between prophet and mystic. The essence of the mystical experience is incommunicable, and resists reduction to the terms of conceptual analytic knowledge. It belongs to the realm of feeling and is incapable of rational adaptation to any recognized system of knowledge. Generally speaking, the mystic cannot offer to humanity any fresh insight into, or any new understanding of, the divine Being: his experience is confined to an intense psychic realization of the presence of a God who is transcendent, unknowable, incomprehensible. The experience is all and leads to nothing beyond itself. But, with the Hebrew prophet, the experience is unimportant compared with the result to which it leads. The *raison d'être* of the prophet is to communicate to his fellow-man the deepened understanding of God's character which springs from the divine initiative in self-revelation. Moreover, despite the suggestiveness of Lindblom's comparison of the two types of literature,[1] the prophetic oracles are very different in kind from the *mémoires* of the mystic. The prophet, unlike the mystic, does not fumblingly and haltingly record the characteristics and the content of a peculiar personal experience: he is concerned to announce authoritatively the living Word which manifests itself in the great movements of history. Whatever be the prophet's personal religious experience, it can never be regarded as an end in itself, since the rôle of the prophet is primarily mediatorial—he is the medium whereby the national God communicates His will to the people. It is not the prophet's personal reaction to the divine Word which

[1] In *Die literarische Gattung der profetischen Literatur*

matters, but its acceptance or rejection by the people with whom he is merged.

The religious consciousness of the mystic is at once more individual, more universal and more anonymous. In the mystical experience proper, all notes of time and place, all that is peculiar to special epochs and cultures, tends to become effaced before the abstract humanity, the intensely individual consciousness of the subject. As the mystics of diverse religious traditions climb the hill that leads to the crowning consummation of the mystical quest, they shed the particularities which mark their starting-point and their paths converge in the essential oneness of the beatific vision which is their reward. Moreover, there is the strongest contrast between the prophet's rich subjectivity and the mystic's emptying of his soul, just as there is between the changing and manifold reactions of the Hebrew God and the impassibility of the transcendent One who is the Object of the mystical consciousness.

It is also impossible to deny the eminent rationality of prophetic discourse. The prophets show themselves to be sane, logical, and lucid, and to be equipped with dialectical powers which render them expert in controversy. They exhibit an intellectual grasp which permits them to comprehend and elicit the most far-reaching implications of the positions they take up. In his passion for drawing the logical consequences, Amos revolutionizes the current eschatology; and his massive perception of the centrality of ethics in religion seems to carry him so far as to make him suggest that a sacrificial cultus of any kind is a regrettable declension from the more purely spiritual ideal of nomadic religion (5: 18 ff., 25). Yet reason is not the ultimate source of the truths which the prophets inculcate. How came Isaiah to realize that Yahwe securely controlled the brutal might of Assyria when the plain verdict of history seemed to belie such a notion? How did Amos become so acutely aware that Yahwe purposed to destroy Israel when such a conviction was revolting alike to the reason and the religious beliefs of his contemporaries? How could Jeremiah be so utterly certain that the victory of the Chaldeans proceeded from Yahwe's intention to punish Israel, and not, as might have been supposed, from the superior power of the gods of Babylon? How could the monotheistic faith be developed and perfected by Deutero-Isaiah in face of the disasters of the Exile which naturally prompted the puzzled question: Where is their God? (Ps. 79: 10).

These questions can be answered only when we realize that the ultimate ground of the prophetic consciousness consists in an immediate and experimental knowledge of God. If it be objected that this is to entangle the prophetic consciousness in our modern subjectivity, whereas the real *locus* of prophetic revelation is the external event, we would reply that the adequate appreciation of such revelatory events depends upon the divine illumination of the prophet's mind under the impact of his communion with God. Again, if the root of the prophetic consciousness be sought in such unusual psychic phenomena as ecstatic audition, vision, and dream, it is easy to show that such psychical accompaniments of the prophetic message are a mere mental mechanism which may become the vehicle of truth or falsehood according to the inner character of the experient.

Thus we are thrown back upon that which constitutes the fontal spring of all prophetic truth, viz., the soul's confrontation by the living God in the deepest zone of its life. This experience is central and determinative of all else. The relation between the reasoned development of prophetic discourse and the governing intuition on which it rests is illuminated by the psychological mechanism of creative inspiration which we have sketched. The prophetic oracle proceeds from such an intensification of consciousness as ultimately enhances and quickens all the faculties of the mind. But everything flows from this original personal apprehension in which the soul becomes vividly aware of the presence and character of its God. Only in this way can we account for the genesis in the prophet's mind of those truths—the omnipotent righteousness of the one God—which become the foundation of all his subsequent thinking. Such theological truths are not the conclusion of a process of philosophic thought; they are the logical implicate of an intuitive consciousness of God as the ultimate and abiding Reality in whom all things cohere. Among the prophets, only Isaiah has given us anything approaching an explicit account of such an experience, and in the description of his inaugural vision we catch a glimpse of the deep creative sources of the prophetic faith. For here we see, first, such an august revelation of the majesty, the infinite power and reality of God that the soul shrinks in shuddering awe, and yet glows under this flaming apprehension of the divine. It pours itself out in such utter self-identification with God that, speaking from the standpoint of modern psychology, we could characterize the experience as an ecstatic bursting asunder of soul and body. Secondly, we have the soul's equally intense realization of the divine holiness which reacts as consuming wrath at the contact of the unclean. It knows itself to be standing, abashed and self-condemned, before One who is infinitely holy and in whose presence sin cannot dwell. The prophet goes away from such an experience conscious of having approached the inmost shrine of divinity, and possessing a conviction which thenceforth masters his personality and fills his mental horizon with an unforgettable vision of the divine.

In this unitive knowledge of God, which all the prophets shared, the eternal reality of God confronts the soul with such majestic potency as to evoke from it a decisive act of trust and self-commitment. Of this eternal divine Reality, the doctrine of ethical monotheism is simply the translation into metaphysical terms. To suppose that there could be a rival to this living God who had laid hold of their lives with such an overwhelming revelation of numinous power would have been an intolerable stultification of the prophets' experience. The warmth, the intimacy, the vividness of their religious communion were such that they knew themselves to be in vital contact with the Eternal Reality; with that which had the solid durability of the everlasting hills, the impregnability of a fortress, the massive strength of the rocks. This living God filled the universe with His power and presence and was the supreme controlling fact of their lives. They would have echoed the Psalmist's words: "Whom have I in heaven but Thee and there is none upon earth that I desire beside Thee. My flesh and my heart faileth, but God is the strength of my heart and my portion for ever" (Ps. 73: 25, 26).

Whether we consider that, in virtue of this central governing experience, the prophets should be classed as mystics and ecstatics is mainly a question of terminology. It has been our contention throughout that the prophets never rely upon manticism or upon any mere psychological phenomena as an authenticating mark of the validity of their religious communion. The Word that is spoken to them is never automatically conveyed by any particular form of consciousness. For its realization in the inmost depths of the heart, reflection, intuition, holiness of life, the spiritual wrestling of prayer, are man's necessary contribution. This, however, is not to deny all connexion between the prophet and the ecstatic. We have seen that the historical development of Hebrew prophecy was stimulated and re-orientated by the movement of ecstasy in Syria in the days of the early monarchy —alien as this was in several important respects from the traditions of Israel and the characteristics of her native religious consciousness—and it is certain that some of the great prophets gained their insight into fresh ranges of truth in moments of ecstatic rapture or in the stress and tension of unusual psychological states. Nevertheless, in the majority of cases, the ecstasy of the Hebrew prophet is not so much a pathological abnormality, nor the dissolution of his human personality in an overwhelmingly invasive divine afflatus, but such a quickening and intensification of consciousness as permits the spirit of man to grasp the truth with maximum vividness and awareness.

Apart from the question of ecstasy, the prophetic consciousness shares the immediacy and intensity which characterize the mystic's apprehension of God. It is *Dieu sensible au cœur*—God as a heartfelt Reality—whom the prophet knows as Creator, Inspirer, Redeemer, of his whole outlook and experience; and his consciousness, viewed psychologically, is illuminated by those characteristics of artistic inspiration and mystical enhancement of being which we have just sketched. But it is important that we should not proceed to make an unqualified identification of prophet and mystic. For mysticism presupposes a philosophy of religion which is the very reverse of that implied in the prophetic consciousness. Mysticism negates history and its natural term of development is absorption in the deity or the deification of man. The mystic aspires to lift himself above the realm of the manifold and turns away from the turmoil and travail of human life. The very *raison d'être* of the prophet, however, is that he finds divine truth supremely relevant to the drama of a given historical situation. The absolute Reality which breaks in upon him with constraining force is directed towards the movements of history and the conduct of men in the here-and-now urgencies and exigencies of human life. Whereas mysticism, of all forms of the religious consciousness, is the one which is least dependent upon sacramental media, the prophetic consciousness, by its profound vision of the metaphysical significance of time and of earthly realities, may be said to prepare the way for the Incarnation and the sacramental values implicit in Christianity. It supplies the key to the understanding of the religious mission and the originality of Israel from Moses to Jesus. The prophet in his vision bridges the gulf which classical antiquity for the most part postulates between God and the world, for, whereas in most of the religions and philosophies of ancient times God is conceived as the unmoved object of man's quest, here God is apprehended as being Himself in quest of man and as yearning in passion and pain for the response of His wayward child.

PART TWO

THEOLOGY

Chapter One

REVELATION AND AUTHORITY

(i)

IN the preceding section we have made a psychological analysis of the character of prophetic experience, and we have shown that, though far removed from mystical absorption, it may be legitimately interpreted as a variety of that immediate and experimental knowledge of God which is claimed by all the mystics. We have now to raise the question as to what constitutes the metaphysical validity of this immediate apprehension of God, and what authority may be accorded to the confident affirmations in which it issues. A psychological analysis of the prophetic consciousness can do little more than elucidate the mental mechanism operative in those crisis-states in which the prophet believes himself to be the recipient of the Word of God. Psychological analysis is applicable strictly to the form in which the message is received: the truth or falsehood of the message itself must be decided by general philosophical considerations. To such, we now turn.

But we cannot determine the nature of the authority to which the prophetic utterances may lay claim without first examining the meaning of revelation and its philosophical basis. "No prophecy ever came by the will of man: but men spake from God, being moved by the Holy Ghost" (2 Pet. 1: 21). Our task is to discover the metaphysic implied by this declaration of religious faith. What do we mean by saying that God spake to the prophets; or, in other words, what is the metaphysical character of the prophets' knowledge of God? The older view, that revelation consists in the divine impartation of transcendent truth undiscoverable by the unaided human reason, can no longer be maintained. It contradicts our general understanding of the nature of God and man, and the relations that obtain between them. It implies the magical and impersonal manipulation of human personality such as would defeat the divine purpose in creation, or else it presupposes in the recipient of the revelation a mind as infinite in capacity as that of the Revealer. Quite apart from these philosophical objections, however, such a conception of revelation is shattered by an impartial scrutiny of the facts and of the exact character of Hebrew prophecy. A study of the record of prophetic revelation shows at once that the prophets were not at all concerned to convey abstract dogmatic truth concerning the nature of the divine being: they were not the exponents of inscrutable mysteries supernaturally revealed. The truth which they apprehended was practical truth immediately relevant to a given historical situation. What was quite as important as its objectivity, or its correspondence with fact, was the consideration that it "found" them with heart-searching power, exercising over their spirits a gracious compulsion to which they could not but surrender themselves. Its apprehension arose out of the vital constraining impact of the divine Spirit upon the human, revealing itself as eternal personal Will, set in a polar relation to the human will, and evoking a decisive act of obedience, self-commitment and trust. To have reduced this living truth to barren intellectualist formulation would have been, in some measure, to distort it and to weaken its majestic spiritual authority. For it is truth which emerges as something integral to the living fellowship of the soul with God, and it cannot be rightly apprehended or realized by one who stands outside the sphere of that dynamic experience. Its embodiment in human word or institution tends to become a formal objectification, in which the glowing flame of the original passionate apprehension flickers feebly and may even die.

We must regard revelation, then, as the transforming self-disclosure of the ultimate personal Reality to the personal spirit of man, and our metaphysic of the prophetic knowledge of God must be framed in accordance with this definition. The prime basic truth underlying all revelation is that of the subjectivity of God. The prophets never think of God as "He": He is always the "Thou" by whom they are addressed and who conditions all their being and thinking. Since He is the omnipresent Knower, He can never properly become the mere object of their thought, for to think in the third person about another is to imply his temporary absence. But the eternal presence and ever-living activity of God alone make possible the prophet's thought: all his thinking about God must be "existential", i.e., carried out in the face of God and governed by the impact of God upon the soul. This truth will be brought out the more clearly if we consider the radical distinction which separates the prophet's knowledge of God from the knowledge of God which is characteristic of the philosopher, the ecstatic mystic and the primitive man.

For these latter types, God is the object, to the attainment of communion with, or knowledge of which, man's endeavour is directed. For the philosopher, God is the infinite and remote object of pure thought; for the mystic, God is the ineffable goal of a lifelong spiritual quest; for the primitive man, God is the mysterious and capricious Unknown, requiring to be propitiated by the exact performance of sacrificial cultus. The prophetic consciousness, with its implications, presents the most striking contrast to such religious attitudes. For the prophets, God is never the object of man's discovery but the subject of a process of self-revelation and self-communication which challenges the spirit of man. God is the initiator of a process of dialectical communion between man and God. In Hebrew theology and anthropology, it is denied that man has the inherent spiritual capacity to find out God; the impassable barrier which separates man from his Maker can be overcome only by God, who wills that man should be brought into fellowship with Himself and should fulfil the requirements which alone can make such fellowship possible. Hence, God is revealed to the prophets as righteous Will, judging man and challenging him to response, obedience and surrender.

But such is the miraculous intimacy of the divine indwelling in man that this revelation, of which God is the subject, does not present itself to the prophet as something foreign to his own personal outlook. The revelation is objective and it is other than man, yet it is not completely external to man. The revealed truth may spring to birth in the prophet's mind with such a flash of insight as may seem like a discovery of which man is the author. The paradox rests upon the mysterious inclusion of man's life in the all-embracing life of God. There is no Word of God which is not also a word of man, the achievement of his earnest spiritual wrestling; the divine Word spoken by the prophet is necessarily refracted through a human medium, stamped with the marks of time and place, bearing indelibly written upon it the living peculiarities of the invidual who gives it utterance. This intimate blending of human and divine, of nature and grace, in the moment of supreme revelation, results in a final, indissoluble, unanalysable unity. Revelation, therefore, is not something which by its overwhelming numinousness leaves man passive and prostrate before it; but something to the reality of which man, by the active co-operation of his mind and spirit, and by responsive faith, must make an essential contribution. It is for this reason that there exists no mechanically applicable criterion of the genuineness of true prophecy. That which is revealed does not lie naked and open to the eye of any chance wayfarer. It is no tangible and palpable display of the supernatural compelling universal recognition. The substance of the revelation is veiled beneath the common outward forms of historical events and natural objects, and is conveyed only to the eyes and ears that are spiritually quickened and thus receptive of divine suggestions. No dazzling theophany stuns the prophet or convinces him against his will. He is no automaton reporting that which he has seen and heard in mystic trance. The necessary contribution of his mind and heart is indicated in the divine exhortation to Jeremiah that he should sift the precious from the common (15: 19). In the last resort, we see that the prophet must make a creative value-judgment which will be determined by the quality of spiritual insight resident in his personality. The event in which the prophet sees the unfolding of God's purpose is susceptible of another interpretation by minds which have not the prophetic vision of the divine love and wisdom and all-controlling Providence. It is just this blending of outward and inward, of external fact and inner interpretative faith, which goes to constitute the prophetic consciousness that God was being revealed.

The knowledge which characterizes the prophetic consciousness is continuous with, and represents the culmination of, other types of spiritual awareness, for all apprehension of value implies the discovery by mind of something akin to itself in the realm of objective reality. Even our knowledge of things depends upon this intimate blend of mind and its object. Just as much as the prophet's experience of God, it is a duality in unity. It is impossible to separate the bare reality of the thing in itself from the thing as perceived by mind. When we come to consider the nature of artistic perception, we have a still more impressive example of the unity of mind with the object of its cognition, for beauty, though it inheres in the form in which it is embodied, yet can only be actualized as it is appreciated by mind. Moreover the artist's apprehension of beauty is a mode of knowledge strikingly analogous to the mode in which the prophet can be said to know God. The poet's commerce with Nature is a spiritual communion in which his mind is receptive of spirit akin to itself yet infinitely transcending itself. We sometimes speak of discovering the beauties of Nature, but this manner of expression does not do justice to the overwhelming objectivity of the experience. It would be more true to speak of Spirit revealing itself to man with a sublimity which challenges his awed and wondering appreciation and fills his soul with a divine content. The poet's vision is not the projection of his own longings, but his imaginative realization of the Spirit of beauty which informs the universe. He is active, in so far as his soul is quickened to a heightened intensity of awareness; but he is passive in that he is the awestruck recipient of something objectively given, and to which he must yield himself in reverent submission. Here we have the duality in unity, the interaction of mind with the self-revealing Other, which is the very hall-mark of revelational knowledge.

Perhaps the closest analogue to the mode of the prophet's knowledge of God is furnished by the knowledge which human persons have of each other. Here, the activity of the mind in discovering the nature of its object is conditioned by the measure in which that object is willing to reveal itself. The distinctive note in our apprehension of other personal selves is the consciousness that we are confronted by a will which, in its spontaneous self-revealing activity, meets our own will with a resistant quality which we cannot dissolve or ignore. We are in contact with an object which we may not dissect and manipulate as we please, but which revolves upon its own mysterious and inaccessible centre of creative life. It impinges upon us in a way which we could not precisely forecast, and our knowledge of it is never complete because in its continuous reaction with its environment it is ever bringing forth fresh revelations of itself from the unfathomable sources of life within.

In all these types of knowledge—sense-perception, the awareness of beauty, and the knowledge of other selves—the mind of the knower combines activity with passivity. He is passive because he encounters an intrusive reality which no mental construction of his own could possibly have created; he is active because a high degree of mental alertness is required for the adequate recognition and appreciation of the character of the reality thus intruded upon his notice. Exactly the same process of knowing is involved in the prophet's awareness of revealed truth. His mode of apprehension is not a supernatural mystery utterly disparate from the normal mental activities in which men take cognizance of the objects and persons by which they are surrounded. Here, as in the psychology of prophecy, the rigid distinction between supernatural and natural, abnormal and normal, is seen to be a false one. We pass, by almost imperceptible gradations, from the one to the other and the variation is due to the degree of intensity to which consciousness is raised and the character of the object apprehended. In the revelational experience of the prophet we reach the culmination of this process of knowing, because there the object which challenges the attention of the prophet is eternal and infinite and requires for its appreciation a consciousness quickened in the highest degree. The prophet's passivity and self-surrender in face of the overwhelming glory of the revelation is naturally more prominent in the record than the stimulation of his faculties for the supreme act of exalted apprehension. But, in fact, the passive and the active aspects of the experience should not be thus separated for they are correlative, each involving the other.

The fact that the subject of the revelation made to the prophet is none other than the eternal God, in whom we live and move and have our being, means that this supreme knowledge transcends and includes all lower degrees of knowledge. Here, we come upon the important principle of mediation. The God with whom the prophets have to do is One whose presence they cannot escape. Since He is the omnipresent spiritual Reality immanent in all things, there is nothing in the whole range of their experiences which cannot become the medium of His approach. In every contact, whether with the world of nature or the life of man, they are awed and subdued by the tokens of His presence. They are conscious that at any moment, and in any perception, they may be addressed by the eternal Thou. The whole context of their life in its perpetually enriched store of impressions and sensations is a shimmering transparent vesture through which shines the eternal Spirit. The finger of God touches them at every turn. This explains the important rôle which sense-perception assumes as a creative source of suggestion in Hebrew prophecy. The high and holy One may use the humblest of earthly media in order to make known His will unto His servants the prophets. The enhancement of consciousness which we have shown to be the characteristic mark of prophetic inspiration implies as its necessary corollary an enhancement of sense-perception, since the animated body, in Hebrew anthropology, is the essential organ of personality. Revelation rests upon the enormously quickened psycho-physical receptiveness and responsiveness of the prophet's whole man. Hence we find that usually the creative nucleus of the prophet's revealed message consists in some illuminating suggestion mediated through sensuous activity—often apparently casual visual perception.

(ii)

It has been necessary to discuss at some length the character and implications of the revelation vouchsafed to the Hebrew prophets, in order that we may be in a position to determine the nature of the authority which their deliverances may claim. It will have become obvious from our treatment of the subject that, in our view, the authority of prophecy does not consist in verbal oracles supernaturally imparted, but rather in the inspired potency and quality of the prophet's living experience of God. The prophet is distinguished from his fellow men by his unusual capacity to make vivid and luminous contacts with Ultimate Reality. The authority to which he is entitled is the authority which inheres in all genius. The unequal endowment of men is a fact which is universally acknowledged, and there is no reason to conclude that it should not obtain, in religion, as well as in the other fields of human activity. We have to trust the declarations of men of genius as to whether a given work of art is or is not beautiful, and we know that our trust is warranted because we feel that they have a more penetrating insight and a finer sensitiveness to the spirit of beauty than is commonly found among men. But it may be objected that the prophets' revelations cannot possess authority for reasonable men just because of their exceptional character, because they are not discoverable by the universal reason of man. There is no answer to this rationalist objection except to say that the ratiocinative processes of the intellect are not the only method of apprehending truth. The insight into and the imaginative creation of beauty are equally far removed from the principles of rational speculation. Yet no one should for that reason reject the validity of the artist's æsthetic consciousness or fail to see that, by the method of imagination, he is apprehending a value which is of ultimate significance for mind. There is simply no *rapport* between the experiential knowledge of value and the inferential discovery of truth.

Our whole argument has been that in the prophetic consciousness we find the experimental, as opposed to the speculative, knowledge of God, and that this knowledge is not discontinuous with, but rather is the culminating transcendent point of other kinds of immediate awareness. We have shown that it is one with sense perception, the awareness of beauty and the knowledge of other selves. In all these experiences, we have a direct acquaintance with reality which cannot be dissolved into rational concepts nor exhaustively explained in terms of reason. We are face to face with the mystery of something given, endowed with all the rich concreteness of the individual and the particular—something whose existence we cannot but acknowledge as the limiting data and the ultimate criterion of all our thought. The confused wealth of concrete reality which we are for ever apprehending by the organs of sense can never, properly speaking, be understood by reason. No satisfying explanation can ever be given as to why the individual thing should exist in the precise character in which we perceive it to exist. The simplest object of perception is just as great a mystery to the intellect as the supreme revelations of truth and beauty accorded to prophet and poet. The inquiring intellect may tabulate and classify phenomena and may determine their causation, but this is very different from giving an ultimate *reason* as to why the chain of causation should be such as it is and not otherwise. The reason which ever aspires to comprehend can only do so at the cost of an abstracting analysis in which the peculiar characteristics of reality as experienced are evaporated. Only by the imagination of the poet, as opposed to the reason of the philosopher, can the original quality of the experience be adequately conveyed to another.

The fact, therefore, that the prophetic knowledge of God is not amenable to the principles of reason cannot be considered to invalidate it, for the character of that knowledge is such as to make it inadmissible to regard reason as the appropriate test of its validity. Instead of being themselves judged by reason, the intuitions of the prophetic consciousness may rightfully claim to exercise an authoritative control over the speculations of reason itself. We have pointed out that the thought of a Jeremiah, for example, might well have been regarded by his contemporaries as offering a flagrant contradiction to practical wisdom and the inferences of rational judgment. What principle, then, may be held to furnish a true test of the validity of the prophetic utterances? In other words, what is the ground of the authority which may be assigned to the religious consciousness of man?

There is no such universal principle which can be mechanically applied as a test, for the simple reason that only the Spirit of God can know the things of God,[1] and that man can appropriate them and acknowledge their truth only in so far as he is a partaker of the divine nature. The authority of the prophetic utterances is a spiritual and intrinsic authority. It cannot be established merely by reason, nor by anything external to itself, such as the peculiar manner in which it may have entered into the prophet's consciousness. The authority of the

[1] i Cor. 2: 11

revelational truth resides in the primal fact which constitutes it as such, viz., the fact that it springs from the
impact of the divine upon the human spirit. But such
truth can never be demonstrated or argued. It must win
spontaneous recognition by its own self-evidencing
power. It "finds" us, as Coleridge put it,[1] that is, it
evokes in us an attitude of reverent submission in which
the spirit of man bows before the authority of the Spirit
of God. In so far as we appreciate the truth of the prophetic utterance, we become sharers in the spiritual
experience through which it was mediated. If we stood
entirely outside that experience we could never recognize
the truth which is integral to it. Our recognition of the
validity of the prophetic revelation is thus not a judgment
of the intellect but the surrender of the soul which
inclines before the freely apprehended good. It is a
moral and spiritual decision of the will submitting itself
to the demand of God mediated through the words of
Holy Scripture. These words should be regarded not as
the words of the rationalist exponent of truth, but rather
as the electrically charged words of the poet. Their
function is not merely to convey conceptual truth, but
to radiate to our souls the dynamic quality of the experience which generates them. They are the vehicle through
which the haunting spiritual potency of the original
revelation reverberates through the souls of those who
submit themselves to its sway. This is what the Reformers
meant by their important doctrine of the *Testimonium
Spiritus Sancti Internum.* To some extent, they objectified
the authority of the Spirit by chaining it to the verbal
media through which it was expressed. But, by their
doctrine of the *Testimonium Spiritus Sancti Internum,* they
corrected the deadening tendency of authoritarianism
and re-established the inwardness of the ever-living
Spirit. God alone can bear witness to Himself, and the
Spirit which spake by the prophets must penetrate our
hearts in order to enable us to recognize its living presence and authority in the words of the prophets. This is

[1] Quoted in art. *"Ko Amar Yahwe,"* by W. H. Robinson, *ZATW,* 1923, p. 11

not to say that man is devoid of any *Anknüpfungspunkt* from the standpoint of which he can appreciate the intrinsic power of divine revelation. But his response to the Word of God is not originated by any faculty which he may possess as a permanent and independent endowment of his human nature statically conceived; it is rather to be considered as a *Nachwirkung* of a state of Grace from which he has fallen—a response initiated by the ever-active divine Spirit immanent within him, and continuously moulding his so-called nature by its vitalizing breath.

Chapter Two

THE NATURE OF MAN AND
ITS RELATION TO GOD

IN the previous chapter we have shown, first, that divine revelation is related to the prophet's essential personality in the most intimate and vital manner conceivable; and, secondly, that in responding to the Word of God thus revealed we are *ipso facto* made sharers of the divine life and activity mediated through the prophetic consciousness. These results have obvious implications for our conception of human nature and the character of its relation to the divine. It is now our purpose to draw out these implications.

In the course of our argument we have maintained that the dominant characteristic of the prophetic experience in the moment of apprehended revelation is the final unanalysable unity of the human spirit with the divine. The completeness of this unity suggests that there exists a certain fundamental kinship between man and his Maker—a suggestion which is entirely confirmed by the insistence of the Hebrew Bible upon the theomorphic aspect of man's being. The question which we have to consider is whether the prophetic consciousness throws any light upon the exact nature of this kinship and that which consitutes it.

At first sight, it might seem that this Biblical emphasis upon man's resemblance to God were contradicted by another thought which is equally distinctive of Hebrew theology, viz., that of the impassable gulf which separates the Creator from the creature. For the Hebrew, God dwells at an infinite height, and man looks up to Him from below: the Hebrew does not, like the Indian mystic, discover God by plumbing the inner depths of his soul. Hence, it would seem that the Hebrew soil was most unfavourable for the growth and realization of the idea that man is like God and may even, in moments of inspiration, participate in the divine life. Let us consider, first, the doctrine of divine immanence in man, or man's affinity to God, as this has sometimes been held, and then review, in the light of it, the data furnished by the prophetic consciousness.

In the philosophy of Western mysticism it has been contended that the soul of man partakes of the substance of divinity. This notion, for example, is clearly expressed in Eckhart's teaching on the *Seelengrund*. According to Eckhart, the apex of the soul is a spark which is so akin to God as to be one with Him.[1] Its intrinsic divinity is such that it would be more correct to describe it as being of the substance of God than as being united to God. It is significant that he should consider it appropriate to characterize the divinity of this spark by precisely those terms which he applies to the transcendent and the absolute. Thus, the divine ground of the soul is nameless, ineffable, transcending all distinctions. It is satisfied only with the superessential essence which lies beyond the particular manifestations of Father, Son, and Holy Ghost.[2]

Now, whatever be the doctrine of divine immanence which a consideration of the prophetic religious experience leads us to formulate, it will not be expressed in such terms as these, for this teaching reposes upon presuppositions which are in radical conflict with the Hebrew understanding of man. It is impossible to reconcile this idea of the intrinsic divinity of the soul with the *données* of Hebrew anthropology which, as we have seen, excludes the notion that the soul is a separate and self-subsistent entity. The teaching of Eckhart really presupposes the dualism of Greek anthropology. On all such views of man and his relation to God, the soul is conceived as a particle of divinity, temporarily detached from its source and lodged within the animal body of man. It is obvious that the doctrine of immanence which the Hebrew prophetic consciousness implies is something very different from this.

[1] Inge, *Christian Mysticism*, p. 156   [2] *op. cit.*, pp. 157, 158

We must go back to the form and structure of the prophetic experience. The Word of God, we have contended, is mysteriously inwrought into the words of frail and finite man, and so complete is this fusion that it is impossible to separate the two. Divine immanence must be so conceived as to allow for this creative unity in duality. The divine Word is objective, in that it is truly God who is expressed, and not the thoughts of man's heart; but it is subjectively conditioned, in that it emerges luminously, as something integral to the total context of the prophet's human experience—an experience which he regards as essentially revelatory. The truth which the prophets declare is apprehended through passion and pain. The personal sorrows of Hosea unfold to his wondering gaze the tragic drama which is being wrought out in eternity. Jeremiah learns the secret of the divine pathos as he wrestles through the long dark night of his soul, with some mysterious angelic visitant. Now, the fact that the personal experience of the prophet is of this revealing and illuminating quality implies that the larger all-embracing personal life of God flows through it and at the same time contains it. God does not stand over against the prophet, as one distinct object stands over against another, for this would mean that the prophet is external to God, and that God is less than the Absolute which comprehends all things. God the transcendent Other is also the mysteriously near, ceaselessly working from within man's life which is taken up into His own. The divine activity at the heart of human life is none other than that constraining impact of God upon the soul which we have defined as the very essence of revelational experience. The objective divine demand which "stabs the spirit broad awake" and evokes a decisive response is something which man can immediately recognize as the transcendent good. He recognizes it because it presents itself to him as being unmistakably akin to that which is already ineffaceably written on his heart. But this act of recognition and response, in which the prophet appropriates truth through personal passion, is not to be conceived as an act initiated by a static and self-contained human nature. It is only possible because of the basic priority of the divine initiative preventing man, and enabling him to make the right response to his Maker. The response of surrender, which makes the prophet what he is, takes its origin in the creative activity of the living God who is dramatically immanent within the soul. Were it not so, man's soul would still be an autonomous entity, the master of its fate, lying helplessly imprisoned in the bondage of its own self-centredness. God would not then be truly immanent and omnipotent. A hard impervious core of being would lie outside the domain of His control, feeling neither His love nor His wrath. A true doctrine of immanence and omnipotence requires that God should be conceived as prior to, and determinative of, every movement in which the soul is propelled towards the good.

This inclusion of man in the life of God does not involve any loss or absorption of individuality: it means rather its enhancement and enrichment. The prophets are never more truly themselves than when they are speaking with the voice of God. Then the firm outlines of their personalities stand out even more sharply. We cannot fail to be arrested by the passionate rectitude of Amos; the rich emotional sympathy of Hosea; the placid wisdom of Isaiah; the eager poetic sensitiveness of Jeremiah; the fierce asceticism of Ezekiel. Similarly, when St. Paul's words seem to be most fully upborne by the current of divine inspiration, as for example in his Epistle to the Romans, the formative elements of his culture—his Rabbinic dialectics and his Hellenic science —are most richly exploited and realized. All is of God, and yet it is just when the prophet submits in utter dependence upon God to become a channel of communication for the divine will that his personality finds its freest and fullest self-expression.

The doctrine of divine immanence which we are thus led to formulate differs radically from that proper to pantheistic mysticism. The immanence which the prophetic consciousness implies may not be interpreted simply as the divine seal set upon an independent human nature, or as divinity once for all infused into the ground of the soul. It is something very much more dynamic and creative than the common immanentist notion that the divine is diffused on a graduated scale throughout the ladder of creation and that this diffusion of the divine becomes most intense in the mind of man. This notion does not do justice to Hebrew anthropology and the Hebrew idea of the *ruach* of God, apart from which prophetic experience cannot be understood. It presupposes that there exists in "human nature" (statically conceived) some part, whether we call it mind, soul, or spirit, which is in itself a pure reflex of the divine. But the primitive Hebrew conception of man cannot make room for such a presupposition. It is true that in post-exilic times, as a result of the accumulated store of prophetic religious experience, the divine supernatural *ruach* became acclimatized in man's life, and the term was used to denote the higher spiritual phenomena which formerly had been ascribed to the *nephesh*. But this modification does not really affect the fundamental Hebrew understanding of man as a complex of physical organs made into a living unified whole by the inbreathing of the breath of Yahwe. The simple unity of this conception was never lost. Man's personality was always identified with the animated body; hence, it was always conceived as an indivisible organism functioning as an integrated unity. There was no finished and self-contained human nature with its higher and lower planes of life. There was no conception of humanity as possessing, intrinsically and permanently, by virtue of its very constitution, the faculties of reason and spirit which might betoken its divine origin. Man was no self-explanatory being operating in accordance with the law of some clear and definable mechanism. There was no nature of man at all understood as something given. Man did not emerge as a finished product from the hands of his Creator, capable of running thenceforth as a machine. He was considered rather as plastic and amorphous material ever accessible to divine invasion from without. His achievements in the moral and spiritual field were not attributed to the working of some self-sufficient implanted faculty, but rather to the invasion of the divine *ruach* taking possession of some one physical organ. Man was nothing in himself, and apart from his fashioning by God's continuous creative activity. Here we reach the deepest truth of Hebrew anthropology, which consists in the suggestion of man's essential nothingness and perishability in so far as he stands in isolation from the creative breath of God. His dignity and *humanitas* lie in his inescapable relatedness to God. A man's wholeness (*shalom*) is conditioned by the fact that the breath of God is in his nostrils (Job 27: 3), that he draws deep from the inexhaustible fountain of life which lies within the mysteries of God's being. But when God withdraws His Spirit from man and rebukes him in wrath and indignation, then the entire psycho-physical frame of man's life suffers eclipse, becomes distorted by disease and seems about to sink into the gulf of death (Ps. 102).

Such is the circle of ideas which we have constantly to bear in mind in defining the character of the kinship between man and God which the prophetic consciousness implies. That kinship must be interpreted in terms of dynamic relation between the divine and the human. Man has no divine soul-substance. He is not endowed with any fixed nature constitutive of his resemblance to God. He is a frail creature of dust, but he is capable of being used as a vehicle for the manifestation of the divine. The true end of his life is not deification but the embodiment and realization of a divine meaning. His uniqueness lies in his addressability by God, his capacity to receive and express in human terms the divine Word. It is precisely in his becoming vitally related to God through his responsive surrender to the divine demand that he actualizes his kinship with God and elicits the divine image within him. The prophets were aware of

God as summoning, upholding and judging them. The supreme factor of their experience was this awareness of confrontation by the divine Word embodying itself in the sacramental media of their multitudinous contacts with life. The divine impinged upon them from without: it did not spring up from the inner depths of their souls. Man had no permanent independent endowment in virtue of which he was able, on his own initiative, to link himself to God.

The immanence which the prophetic consciousness implies may best be expressed by speaking of the "theological structure" of man's being. Man is constructed in such a way that the supposition of his relatedness to God offers the only satisfying explanation of his deepest characteristics. As Pascal argues,[1] unless we place him in the dimension of the eternal living God, he appears as a monstrous, enigmatic chimera. His nature is no clear-cut mechanism containing its principle of explanation within itself. It is a finite focus in space and time for the appreciation of values which are infinite and eternal. It is a mysterious centre of hidden incalculable potentialities for good and ill. One of the thoughts which emerges most prominently from the background of Hebraic theology is that of the creativity of God and the createdness of man. As we have seen, this thought determines Hebrew anthropology. It should also control our interpretation of the light which the prophetic consciousness throws upon the nature of man. But the creativity of God is a continuous process, and man's distinctive prerogative among the creatures is seen in the fact that he does not come forth as a completed article from the divine workshop. His characteristic humanity does not reside in any irrevocably given faculty, but is something which can only be realized by living and dramatic intercourse with his Creator. His resemblance to God springs from his inalienable capacity for such dynamic fellowship. Immanence therefore means, not that God is mirrored in some independently operative human

[1] *Pensées*, p. 531

faculty, but that God the infinite transcendent Subject is the omnipotent controller of that dramatic spiritual relationship in which man realizes himself as he responds to the decisive address of the eternal Thou.

Chapter Three

THE PERSONALITY OF GOD

PERHAPS the most vital theological implication of the prophetic consciousness is that of the personal existence of God. This implication is central and dominant, determining all the others. The conception of God as a living agent whose activity is seen in the historical process depends upon the ascription to Him of creative Will, and creative Will can be postulated only of personality. That mutual interaction of time and eternity which is the basic assumption of the prophetic faith—a fundamental original insight which has moulded the whole theological outlook of the Jewish-Christian religious tradition—is thus inextricably linked with the idea of God as living Will, Will being necessarily correlated with time. Again, the doctrine of God as "pathetic", as sharing the sufferings of the world and bearing the burdens of His frail and finite creatures, likewise rests upon the implicit notion that His mode of existence is analogous with that of man, at least includes within itself the highest levels of being to which man has attained. We may say, then, that the personality of God is the keystone in the arch of the theological structure which may be built out of the implications of the prophetic consciousness.

The prophetic consciousness may be interpreted as the constraining pressure exercised by absolute moral values over the human spirit. The prophets are urged to prophesy because they perceive that such values are being defied and negated in the conduct of their contemporaries. They are constrained by the dictates of moral conscience, and they apprehend this inward spiritual pressure as the coercive touch of God upon their soul. They feel themselves to be confronted by the unconditioned demand of God who is revealed as personal holy Will.

In this basic characteristic of their religious experience we have something which necessarily implies personality in the God who determines and inspires it. These values, which wield such overpowering and authoritative sway upon the spirit of man, prove by their very nature that they are ultimate and are rooted in objective reality. They cannot be the mere projection of man's interior idealism and longing, for they set up an invincible resistance to the human will which seeks to evade their impact. If they were but the externalization of man's inward struggles, then they would lose their characteristic tone-colour. They would no longer be felt as an awful impassable barrier fixing a limit to the free play of the soul's life. Any self-imposed limit to man's desires is always removable at will; but the characteristic quality of the resistance offered by these ultimate values springs from the fact that they constitute an absolutely irremovable frontier, thrusting itself into the heart of human life from the outside. Against such a frontier man chafes in vain and, in violating it, hurls himself to destruction. Thus, his very apprehension of these values is the apprehension of something objectively real, an integral part of the constitution of ultimate reality to which man must adjust himself if he would attain security and well-being.

Now the nature of value is such that it must centre in persons. Value has significance and relevance for personality alone. The law of nature, which is descriptive, holds for the physical universe; the moral law, which is imperative, holds only for a world of persons, and demands that its source and sustainer should be personal Spirit. The validity of values does not spring from their realization in the lives of the personal beings for whom they are valid. Rather, the personality of these beings is realized in the very process of striving to embody the value which they apprehend. Value judges us; it is other than ourselves; it is felt as impinging upon us from the outside. Its ultimate source must, therefore, be the inmost nature of the Reality in a right reaction to which we grow into the fullness of our personal stature. This can only mean that God is personal. The values which the prophet apprehends are such as to evoke an attitude of reverence, submission and trust, and this attitude is only intelligible on the assumption that its Ground has personal nature.

A second line of argument for personality in God starts likewise from the special character of the religious experience of the prophets. That experience is essentially a unity in duality. The prophets are conscious of standing in a personal relationship to the divine encountered in life's common way. This divine Reality addresses them as persons, makes demands upon them, expresses itself in the tension which characterizes a living Will. When the prophet feels the approach of his God, he is conscious of entering into a realm of personal relationships, where wills confront each other in their irreducible exclusiveness, where separate centres of consciousness meet. The achievement of fellowship with God is no interpenetration of the prophet's mind and heart by a kind of pervasive impersonal influence, but an act of self-surrender and voluntary union with the Other, whereby the very climax of personality—self-transcendence—is attained. The fellowship achieved pre-supposes an original difference overcome, and the union of wills, as a result of which the prophet lives in and for God alone, means not the mere annihilation of distinctions, but the enrichment and enhancement of the prophet's distinct individuality. This salient characteristic of the prophet's religious experience will be thrown into relief if we compare and contrast it with other types of religious communion which repose upon different theological presuppositions. It is untrue to say that all genuine religious experience requires that we should postulate a personal God as its Object. Everything depends upon the precise character of the experience. It is very possible for mystical states to arise in which the soul is thrilled with an almost painful joy or trembles with shuddering awe under the consciousness of a numinous Presence. These are mystical moments *par excellence* when the soul feels itself to be swept by the inmost breath of Reality, to be enclasped securely in the bosom of the All. In such moods, the soul realizes and rejoices in the truth that it is an integral part of the Whole of things: the feeling of separateness vanishes and is replaced by that of absorption in the Absolute. These feeling-states are the special characteristic of certain types of mysticism, in particular those which emanate from or have affinity with oriental religions. But they occur also from time to time in the Christian stream of religious tradition and they give rise to a characteristic theology which contrasts notably with the affirmation or implication of divine personality to be found in the Hebrew prophets. The theology to which we refer is that of the *via negativa* and it consists in negating all specific attributes of the deity. Every particular theological definition is felt to imply a limitation of the transcendent God. Even existence cannot be truly predicated of Him. The One, the Absolute, is above existence. To assert that He exists is to confess that our thought remains entangled in the symbolism derived from human experience. The most outstanding representative and exponent of this negative theology is Dionysius the Areopagite[1] who systematically refuses to apply to God all the highest concepts, such as unity, spirituality, wisdom, goodness, in terms of which the being of God has usually been defined. It is obvious that here we have the polar opposite of the theomorphic argument which emphatically asserts of God His inclusion of the highest humanity has reached. To the negative theology corresponds a peculiar type of religious communion which represents the spiritual development of those vague states of mystical feeling referred to above. Just as the negative theology is the antithesis of the implicit theomorphism of prophetic theology, so the religious experience of these mystics presents us with a marked contrast to the prophet's fellowship with a personal God. Instead of the communion of personal spirits, we have the soul's ecstatic absorption into the

[1] Inge, *Christian Mysticism*, pp. 105 ff.

transcendent One. Instead of the clear-cut outlines of
the prophet's self-affirming personality, which receives
a vast enhancement of being through its responsive
surrender to the personality of God, we have the extreme
asceticism of the mystic who strips himself of every
quality and function of personal life in order to attain
that passionless apathy and emptiness which is the pre-
lude to his deification. It is true that the prophet also
loses himself in self-identification with his God, but it is
precisely through this process of self-surrender that he
realizes positively the potentialities of his individual and
distinct personality. His fundamental identity as a self
is not lost, but rather emerges sharpened and enriched.
Nothing is more characteristic of the prophets than the
rich and concrete individuality which stamps their
utterances and differentiates them unmistakably from
each other. In the mystical type of which we are speaking, personal individuality is felt as a limiting condition;
the mystic aspires, not to self-realization through self-
sacrifice, but to the dissolution of the self in the All. The
most thoroughgoing instance of this species of religious
consciousness is seen in the Buddhist, for whom personal
existence itself is the essential misery from which mankind needs to be delivered. But the same aspiration to
overcome the limits implied in selfhood is an ever-
recurring phenomenon in mystical religion.

The point, however, that we specially desire to
emphasize is that the denial of personality in God is the
exact logical correlate of this religious attitude. For,
instead of a universe of personal spirits reaching their
perfection through their interaction with each other and
with the Infinite Personality who is the focus of them all,
the *Weltanschauung* of the extreme mystic is that of a bare
monism in which personal distinctions are transcended.
To give religious value to personality is to imply that it is
embedded in the very stuff of ultimate Reality. But the
mystic confuses personality with individuality and therefore sees it only as separation and limitation, instead of
as fullness of life. To ascribe personality to the Absolute

would therefore be equivalent to assigning imperfection to that which is by definition the Perfect, the One. Personality, which suggests a community of persons, and leads us to regard the universe as a unity in multiplicity, is a concept which cannot be harmonized with a view of the Absolute as the limitless One.

The prophet's fellowship with God is thus a type of religious experience which centres in personality: without personal life both in man and God, it is utterly inconceivable. The soul's attitude of trust, love and adoration which is the keynote of that experience, presupposes personality and otherness in its Object: for, without the distinctness and contrast between the self and the not-self, which personality implies, how is love and worship possible? That mutual interaction and tension between living wills which characterizes the prophetic intercourse with God is automatically precluded by any kind of philosophic thought which conceives the supreme Reality as the mere totality of individual souls and of everything that is. Hence, for prophetic religion, personality, in man and God, is central. The extreme mystic, on the other hand, whose religious experience cannot be discounted, finds personality a limiting condition to be transcended. For him, personality is contingent upon the created order. It is simply the consequence of the finite individuation of spirits. It is therefore the very mark of imperfection, and as such must be transcended in proportion as the soul reaches the height of being by participation in God. In considering these contrasted attitudes we touch upon the essential paradox which inheres in the notion of personality, and gives rise to important philosophic problems when personality is ascribed to God.

The consciousness of personality arises from the opposition between self and not-self. The individual becomes aware of himself as an individual person by contrasting himself with the external reality which forms his environment and stimulus. *Personal* opinions reflect the self's differentiation from universal realities. But this description of personality as individual self-consciousness is by no means exhaustive. The paradox of the idea of personality consists in the fact that, in its growth and development, personality persistently aspires to negate the conditions of its own existence. In perfect personality the isolation and separation of the self-hood would be completely overcome. Indeed, when we observe personality in action, in its dynamic relation with the not-self, our definition seems to be contradicted. For the realization of personality involves the transcendence of the mere impervious selfhood, in the development of the self's inherently expansive outgoing life, and in imaginative communion with its environment. This growth in personal life provides us with the highest principle of unity that we know, for the finite self, by the enrichment and deepening of its personal life, can become a living focus in which the whole universe is mirrored and embraced. The ultimate supremacy of the category of personal spirit is revealed in the fact that it is capable of unifying and of imposing an intelligible coherence upon the mass of phenomena with which it is presented. The "thinking reed" dominates the vast expanse of matter which is the object of his thought. Not only is personality a unifying centre, but it becomes itself ever more unified as its development continues.

This brief consideration of the idea of personality is sufficient to show that, in its application to God, serious difficulties arise which make understandable the attitude of the mystic. If God is the Absolute in whom all things cohere, can we think of Him as standing over in conscious relationship to, and self-differentiation from, the other—things and persons outside Himself? Again, human personality appears as a process of gradual unification through the surrender of the self in loyalty to some commanding ideal. Personal life is a process of ever-increasing integration by means of purposive activity. But this implies the brute fact of discrepancy between the ideal and the actual which cannot be postulated in the life of God.

We may suppose, however, that the characteristics which mark the development of personality in human life are by no means essential conditions of the fact of personality itself; we may envisage them as imperfections attaching to human personality, which would necessarily be transcended in the perfect personality of God. Furthermore, the category of personality supplies us with an illuminative principle, by means of which to conceive the manner of God's relation to the world. Those systems of philosophy which interpret God as the totality of existence (pantheism) or as a purely immanent idea which first attains self-realization and embodiment in the cosmic process of becoming (Hegelian idealism) do not afford a sufficient basis for the unity of existence. We have to discover a principle which is capable of accounting for the coherent structure of reality. The only such principle of which we are aware is the unity and unifying power of spiritual personality imperfectly realized in man. Only a personal God can be conceived as both transcending and including the world. Man's personal appropriation and unification of surrounding reality furnishes us with a faint adumbration of the manner in which a personal God lends unity to His creation by being Himself immanent within it. Just as man becomes one with the object which he apprehends but does not thereby sacrifice his personal distinctness, so God is immanent in the world while remaining transcendent in personal independence of it.

Finally, it must be frankly admitted that the term "personality" represents a symbolic, rather than an exhaustive description of God's nature. We have to bear in mind the essential inadequacy of all human thought and language when the Object of our thinking is One who judges us and whose self-existent Being stands beyond the reach of the finite mind. Personality, in man, is not a finished product but a process of perpetual striving towards an ideal which alone can give rest to our spirits, but which forever exceeds our grasp. Our own experience of personality affords no real parallel to the incomprehensible inclusion within the divine Person of numberless unique centres of self-consciousness, but such measure of personal sympathy and communion as we have attained may be regarded as the imperfect realization of an ideal, and as pointing upward to the mysterious fullness of personal life in the Godhead.

The concept of personality is a symbol which safeguards that essential implicate of the prophetic experience, viz., the faith that God is *living*. Only such a symbol, expressive of the highest that man has attained in the realm of the spirit, can do justice to the supreme intensity and richness of life which the prophets divine in the God who meets them at the heart of their direct personal experience. This faith requires that the analogy between personality in man and personality in God shall be real. Personality must be "formally" in God. Yet there cannot be an exact equivalence between personality in man and personality in God. The concept is symbolic in the sense that it is an index only to some unfathomable reality which, because it is infinite and absolute, eludes exhaustive and exact formulation in terms drawn from and proper to the finite life of man.

Chapter Four

DIVINE PATHOS

THE prophetic consciousness clearly implies the passibility of the divine being. A recent writer[1] considers that the prophetic sympathy with the divine "pathos" is the very ground of Hebrew prophecy. The prophet sees the conduct of Israel set in the light of the divine countenance and he shares to the fullest degree the passion in the heart of God which this conduct provokes. His prophecy consists in the inspired announcement of this divine pathos. The subject of the revelation made to the prophets is not God in the changeless unity of His inner being, but God as specifically determined by and related to the world. The presupposition of such revelations is that God not only rules the world in the majesty of omnipotence, but reacts emotionally to the world's life. He does not judge men's deeds impassively and with aloofness: His judgment is imbued with the emotion of One to whom those actions are the most intimate and profound concern. God does not stand outside the range of human sorrow and tragic suffering. He is the greatest sufferer of all, because He alone can realize the true spiritual repercussions of the drama of human history. He experiences the ultimate significance of every turn and phase of that drama in the most intimate personal way, and with a lucidity and fullness of comprehension which is impossible to any other, because He alone knows the end from the beginning and can perceive and feel the true spiritual implications of every step in time. The central truth of the theology implicit in the prophetic consciousness is just this *Erlebbarkeit* for God of human life and experience. Since God is perfect goodness, He is the one Being who is capable of feeling to the full the tragedy of the world's

[1] Heschel, *Das profetische Bewusstsein*

138

evil. He is the One whom everything concerns, because He lives in and with the created universe, gathering it up into the heart of His eternal life.

This is most clearly brought out in the prophecies o Deutero-Isaiah, and it can be no accident that the prophet who developed the monotheistic doctrine to its fullest extent should also have realized the philosophical implications of the divine pathos. Yahwe is here pictured as the tender and almighty Bearer of Israel's burdens (Isa. 46). By means of this sublime conception, Yahwe is differentiated from the mere nothingness of the heathen gods. The latter are themselves cumbersome burdens to their weary beasts, and require the support of their worshippers. Yahwe, on the contrary, Himself carries the load of sore agony and trial involved in His creation. He accepts the burdens and responsibilities of self-giving love. With profound insight, Deutero-Isaiah sees that the unity and all-sufficiency of Yahwe involves responsibility towards the sufferings of mankind. He does not hesitate to attribute to Him the creation of the possibility of evil, and he makes Yahwe say in self-sacrificial acceptance of the world's woe: "Hearken unto Me, O house of Jacob, and all the remnant of the house of Israel, which have been borne by Me from the belly, which have been carried from the womb: and even to old age I am he, and even to hoar hairs will I carry you: I have made, and I will bear; yea, I will carry, and will deliver" (Isa. 46: 3, 4).

The supreme importance of the divine pathos in the prophetic vision of God is illustrated by the emotional solidarity which binds the prophet to his God. The emotional consciousness of the prophet is a dim earthly reflection of the emotions which Yahwe experiences in heaven. Thus, in such a passage as that of Jer. 15: 17 ff., we see how the prophet's sympathy with God causes him to feel a sense of spiritual isolation from his kind. He sits alone because of God's hand: he is unable to take part in the joyous festivities of the common life. His being is filled with a wrathful indignation which flows from God.

Yet, though his self-identification with God cuts him off from a full and frank participation in the feelings which animate his countrymen, he cannot be emancipated from the bond that unites him indissolubly to them. His individual life is subsumed beneath the corporate life of the nation. He is both the representative of God before the people and the representative of the people before God. Hence, he feels to a degree shared by no other the tragic poignancy of the estrangement between God and His chosen people. The matter has been well summarized in the statement that the prophet is the mouth of Yahwe open towards the people (Jer. 15: 19) and the eye of the people uplifted towards God (Isa. 29: 16),[1] and it is just this twofold sense in which the category of corporate personality can be applied to him that causes his being to echo to its depths the pathos which fills the heart of God.

The prophetic solidarity with the divine pathos[2] receives its most vivid illustration from the experience of Hosea, the narrative of whose marriage draws its whole significance from this conception. If we accept the literal interpretation of the Biblical account, he would seem to have been commanded to marry a harlot precisely in order that he might realize, with all the force and intensity of individual experience, the manifold fluctuations of the divine pathos which the waywardness of Israel has aroused. Only by feeling personally the agony of frustrated love can the prophet gain a true sympathetic realization of the wound which Israel's disloyalty has inflicted on the love of God. Hence, his declaration of the

---

[1] See W. H. Robinson, *ZATW*, 1923, p. 9

[2] The moral and emotional solidarity between the prophet and God is represented in Hosea by the term ידע (*Yada'*) and would appear to have been conceived by him on the analogy of the intimacy of communion which characterizes the experience of sexual love. The formula—to know God—is of course used to suggest clear spiritual appreciation of God's fundamental requirements, but there inevitably clings to the word something of its old and common Semitic connotation of sexual union. Hence, it indicates also the prophet's tender moral and spiritual communion with his God. The prophet Jeremiah bears the name of God (15: 16) as the woman bears the name of the man in sign of the betrothal between them. In the famous complaint of Chapter 20 he uses legal terms denoting the seduction (פתה) and forcing (חזק) of woman (20: 7). God has enticed and enthralled him and so heavily has the divine Spirit pressed upon him as almost to violate his inner sense of personal freedom

divine word is suffused with the divine emotions. The affirmation of divine judgment and future punishment is penetrated with the tenderest feelings of compassion and grief. Impassioned love, vibrating in reaction to every movement of Israel's life, constitutes the very being of Yahwe. The anger, the sorrow, the pain throbbing in the heart of God are "the sweet sad music" to which Hosea's ear is attuned. Infinite vistas are thus opened upon the unfathomably rich content of the divine experience in its relation to humanity. The bitter disillusionment of God, sounding like a plaintive wail through the prophet's message, is a measure of the fiery intensity of His love. The prophet is wholly God-centred: he considers the apostasy of Israel exclusively from the standpoint of God, and his solidarity with the divine pathos reaches such a point that he intercedes for the punishment of Israel (9: 14).

The same theocentric attitude, vividly disclosing the character of the divine pathos, is revealed in Isaiah's parable of the vineyard (5: 1 ff). The emotional undertones of the story are the divine vexation and disappointment. The prophet's consciousness is wholly imbued with the feelings of God. He remains unmoved by the tragic catastrophe which he announces; we trace in him no mood of sadness or regret springing from the *lachrimæ rerum*. Elsewhere in Isaiah, God is depicted as being wearied and disgusted by the disloyal scepticism and immoral cultus of His people. He hides His face in indignation and sorrow when the Israelites with their sin-stained sacrifices invoke His Name (1: 13 ff.).

The passibility of God is thus an integral element in the consciousness of the prophets. Between the implications of the prophetic consciousness and the affirmations of the traditional classical Christian theology there arises a sharp and irreconcilable opposition. Thomas Aquinas affirms that the very notion of passibility is inconsistent with the perfection of pure being which the term "God" connotes.[1] "*Passio* means the abandonment of some

[1] See *Summa* I, *The Immutability of God*, Quest. IX, Art. I

natural quality and the impress of a quality foreign and adverse."[1] This is incompatible with the definition of God as pure act, since the successive changes involved in the experience of feeling imply potentiality—the present realization of a state of being which in the immediate past existed only potentially. These conceptions are rooted in the Greek idea of God, according to which change, indicating imperfection, is necessarily excluded from the perfect circle of the divine Being. For the Greek, a pathetic reaction in the divine nature seemed also to suggest that God was being subjected to a cause other than Himself. Furthermore, this tenacious repugnance to the idea of divine pathos may be traced to Greek anthropology, with its low estimate of emotion as an inferior element in man, whose agitation clouds the higher life of reason and spirit.

All such considerations spring from a world-view which furnishes the absolute antithesis of Hebrew theology and psychology. The Hebrew, had he thought about the matter, would have rejected the pretention of reason to analyse and define the idea of God. For him, the reason is not an independent faculty at all, but is merged in the unity of his psycho-physical life and by its instinctive insights and responses serves the essentially practical needs of this life. The Hebrew prophet works with *l'esprit de la finesse*; the Greek philosopher with *l'esprit de la géometrie*. The one grasps truth intuitively: the other by ratiocinative speculation. In the prophetic approach, determined by Hebrew psychology, there is no trace of that low valuation of feeling as an element which must be transcended if man is to attain to the height of true being. This is so because the Hebrew never considers man as a being whose life is characterized by a graduated scale of parts. As we have insisted, man, for the Hebrew, is an indivisible unity whose thought is interfused with feeling and whose feeling is inseparable from his thought.

The prophetic ascription of a feeling-consciousness to

---

[1] Mozley, *Impassibility of God*, p. 113

God emphasizes the strong contrast between the God of the prophets and the God of the philosophers. The Hebrew and prophetic insistence upon the impassable gulf which separates the Creator from the creature and which eternally prevents man from discovering God by his own initiative and questing, implies that God is essentially unknowable and inaccessible to frail and mortal man who is but dust. "Verily Thou art a God that hidest Thyself" (Isa. 45: 15). There is such a radical antithesis between the approach of the prophet and that of the philosopher as makes it natural to expect an irreducible tension between the affirmations of the one and the conclusions of the other. When we study the theological implicates of the prophetic consciousness, we become aware of moving in an atmosphere which is wholly at variance with the spirit of theological rationalism. It is as if the prophets enter into a new dimension of which the philosophers take no account. This new dimension is that of living personality which defies interpretation in terms of the categories furnished by the intellect. Life, in its freedom, its mystery, its irreversibility, cannot be rationalized. Its crucial revealing acts are full of logical antinomies which thought cannot do away. How much more, then, is it vain to endeavour to comprehend the infinite life of God solely from the standpoint of those categories which the erring reason of man supplies!

It is the living God with whom the prophets have to do. The soul that stands before Him realizes that it is in the presence of almighty Will, overwhelming, insistent, near. Instead of an intellectual abstraction, evolved out of the involutions of speculative human thought, the God of the prophets is a living empirical Reality by whose awful majesty they are confronted in the stress of their human experience. The prophet is aware of God "pathetically" determined by man—God self-expressed in a specific emotional attitude to the world.

The problem for thought which this outlook raises is

that of a possible unworthy humanization and limitation of God, and in order to investigate this problem we must consider what significance we may attach to the idea of emotion in connexion with the divine. Much confusion has been caused by the supposition that the prophetic theology requires us to think of God as being subject to feeling in much the same way as man is subject to it. Feeling, in man, is often a badge of his misery, servitude and imperfection. Human desire and emotion appear as an ever-restless flux which must be controlled and directed by some unifying purpose capable of bringing order and harmony within. It is obvious that feeling in this sense cannot be postulated of God. It would be unjust and unworthy to suppose that the religious apprehensions of the prophets demand that we should think of God as experiencing love, hate, anger, jealousy, in the way in which these are experienced in the life of humanity. The divine pathos of which the prophets are aware does not imply agitation in the depths of the divine Being, or suggest that God is tragically caught in the network of His own creation. Some of these emotions, such as wrath and jealousy, suggest the religious awareness of the fathomless volcanic energies of the living God. They emphasize and translate the prophets' consciousness that God is overwhelmingly alive, compelling, active. They are analogical, borrowed from the sphere of man's affective life to express—as best human language may—the primitive numinous conception of deity. Yahwe is anthropopathic. His glory manifests itself in annihilating terror, and His titanic emotional energies are poured out like "the fierce flow of desolating lava from a flaming volcano".

This understanding of the feeling-consciousness of God is, however, simply the background against which the originality of the prophets' vision luminously emerges. Divine emotion, thus understood, may be regarded as part of the religious inheritance of the prophets. In their peculiar personal vision, it has another and a deeper meaning. It is a means of expressing their sense that God

is personal, ethical, Will. The emotions which the prophets ascribe to God are to be considered as indicating a
series of volitional attitudes. The divine pathos is the
logical correlative of the divine personality. Volition is
the very fulcrum of personality. It *is* personality in
action. Pathos, in God, is not feeling as contrasted with
clear, cold thought. It is no impulsive movement. It is
the personal expression of the ethical holy being of God.
The divine pathos and the divine holiness run into each
other. The ethical law of which God is the upholder is
no independent system to which God is subordinated as
a mediator: it is grounded in His own perfect personality.
On the one hand, pathos, in God, is not an arbitrary
movement of feeling; and, on the other hand, God cannot be reduced to the stiff abstraction of an ethical idea.
Pathos makes possible manifold forms of relation between
man and God. It indicates that the infinite distance
between man and God is overcome by the loving and
prevenient activity of God Himself. It implies man's
precious worth and significance to his Creator. It suggests that the human and divine personalities are not
utterly disparate and discontinuous. It furnishes the
basis of the most vital and intimate relationship between
the eternal and the temporal, the metaphysical and the
historical. Pathos opens up a vision of the absolute self-
lessness and sacrificial love of God.

The meaning of divine pathos as the necessary correlative of divine personality is seen when we consider it as
the personal reaction of God to human sin. It is strictly
governed by a given time-situation. It is not ultimate to
the being of God. It is the immediate, outward aspect of
the divine love as conditioned by the spiritual attitude
of man. It makes room for the possibility and significance
of man's repentance. It renders the moral government of
the world subjective and personal. It makes possible
prayer and intercession, since God can repent even of an
ethically determined decision, as God was moved to
relent at the supplication of Amos (7: 3, 6). The most
vivid illustration of divine pathos is found in the prophets'

glimpse of a conflict between the mercy and wrath of God. This tragic conflict is most poignantly realized by Hosea. Yahwe is depicted as Himself shrinking from the necessity of breaking out as consuming fire. He recoils before this bitter disappointment to His love. How shall I give thee up, Ephraim? How shall I deliver thee, Israel? (11: 8). His love turning itself into its apparent opposite, becomes destructive fury (13: 7 ff.), yet He pleads with Israel not to expose herself to this explosive discharge of wrath (13: 9). But we cannot realize the true significance of this conflict if we attach to these emotions the meaning which they normally bear in human experience. Wrath is but an expression of divine love in face of man's sin, and means that God punishes in sorrow. It is the personal correlative of righteousness, and the measure of man's worth to God. The apparent conflict reveals suffering at the heart of God. Infinite pain and passion throbbing through the divine Being seem to be reflected in the words *Lo-ammi*, *Lo-ruhamah*, which denote so tragic a contradiction of Yahwe's will. God suffers from the *prima facie* frustration of His loving purpose for man, and the dramatic tension between man and God is reflected in that suffering.

It is not possible here to enter into the vast reach of the philosophic problems which the conception of divine pathos involves. It must suffice to note that the conception is proper to that higher anthropomorphism which is the implicit argument of the prophetic consciousness The highest spiritual achievement of man points upward to the eternal reality of God which it implies and from which it springs. The crown of man's spiritual growth is his attainment of personality with the feeling-tone and the suffering which is inevitably associated with it. The very essence of personal being as we know it is the capacity for sympathetic communion and loving self-identification with the not-self, the ability to live in the lives and to share the rapture and the pain of others. This quality of personal life is most vividly exhibited when love is confronted by the fact of evil, to which its characteristic reaction is sacrificial suffering. Growth in holiness involves as its inevitable consequence an increased capacity to suffer, since the highest level of spirituality is revealed in that passionate love which recklessly puts itself into the place of others, feels the stab of their pain and suffers the shame of their sin. The substitutionary sin-bearing of Yahwe's Servant gathers its spiritual reality and significance from the ardent personal love which prompts it.

If we follow out the theomorphic argument and postulate in God the perfection of personal life which is imperfectly realized in man, we shall conclude that there is an unimaginable togetherness of God and man, that God indwells the lives of His creatures, embracing their finite centres of consciousness with the overflowing fullness of His own divine life and love. This immanence of God in the world means that all the striving, toiling and suffering of humanity enters into the heart of the divine experience. God reacts personally to the sin of man. The prophetic consciousness consists in the poignant awareness of this divine reaction. The prophets introduce us to the vision of a God who experiences as no other can the sharp sting of moral evil (which is an offence against Himself the infinitely holy) and who is forever involved in all its sorrow and redemptively bears its pain. The righteousness of God is not an abstract principle such as would render retribution automatic. It pulsates with passion, and springs from the inmost depths of a perfect personal love which yearns with relentless persistence to make the beloved object worthy of communion with itself. The prophetic consciousness thus implies that the being of God consists, not in a solitary and self-sufficient bliss, but in an overflowing fountain of love and joy which are poured forth upon the created world, without suffering diminution and which go forth in passionate longing to gather man into the circle of divine fellowship. In the fact of God's suffering personal concern for man lies the possibility of atonement, which offers the divine solution to the human problem of sin.

Does the prophetic vision of divine suffering really contradict the twofold thought of God's joyous blessedness in eternity and His omnipotence? If suffering in God implied inability to achieve His purpose through some resistance offered from outside; if it meant the pain and weariness of a struggle whose ultimate issue was uncertain; then, indeed, it might be considered incompatible with the thought of divine omnipotence. The divine pathos which the prophets envision is, however, something very different from the idea of an unhappy and frustrated God subject to impressions from without. So far from suggesting frustration, it is the very means whereby the divine triumph is secured. For the divine pathos implies a reaction to man's sin which, while exhibiting the evil in its true light, effects such a spiritual transmutation of the situation as does away the burden of guilt and the estrangement of man from God that is its necessary consequence. Such a spiritual transfiguration of the fact of evil could be accomplished only by the travail pangs of personal, suffering Spirit. While this theology of divine atoning love is not consciously reached by the prophets, it is the only kind of theology which is compatible with the implicates of their peculiar awareness of God. Hosea comes nearest to its specific formulation, for his own human experience of the costliness of inexorable pardoning love taught him to realize something of the tragic tension which cleaves the heart of Yahwe. All the passion of sacrificial self-abandoning love seems to be distilled into the words: "I will heal their backsliding, I will love them freely; for Mine anger is turned away from them" (14: 4).

Nor does this note of tragic poignancy dim the splendour of divine joy and blessedness. To suppose that it could do so would be to adopt an all too human and hedonistic understanding of felicity. In God, the fire of love is so intense that the sacrificial bearing of man's evil is not consciously felt as pain, but is transfused with purest joy. The pain of sacrifice is lost in the joy of ultimate triumph. This joy is the ground tone of the divine experience, because God feels the time process as a whole, and tastes the untainted blessedness of purpose accomplished. The divine pathos is not mere suffering, because it springs from voluntary self-limitation and is incidental to the unconstrained creative self-expression of the divine love. Through the toil and pain of sacrifice, Love knows itself to be accomplishing its eternal triumph over evil, and this triumph is no contingent event of the future but an eternal act wrought in an eternal now and diffusing the divine glory through the universe.

The possibility of God means that at the heart of the universe is no iron system of law but the winning redemptive Grace (חסד=*hesed*) *of a personal God.* This truth is clearly seen if we contrast the spirituality of Christianity with the law of "Karma" as taught in Eastern religions. Karma expresses the undeviating operation of impersonal justice. Retribution is automatic, the dead weight of the past can only be done away by expiation of sin. This outlook precludes the characteristic notes of Biblical religion, viz. repentance and redemption, the supremacy of personal spirit, the triumph of love over law. Such characteristic effects are grounded in the prophetic conception of God as living personal Energy and Will, the Lover of souls, the Creator, Redeemer and Father of men's spirits, calling men with a persistent, steadfast love to abiding fellowship with Himself. Above all, pathos signifies the high worth of man to God and his centrality in the scheme of creation. *Not only God for man, but man for God is meaningful.* Thus divine pathos points to the possibility of fellowship between man and God on the basis of ethical communion and likeness and prepares the way for the fuller revelation of Christian love, suggesting both a theology and anthropology to which the idea of the Incarnation is appropriate.

The God whose "emotions" the prophets express is not the numinous, the wholly other, but the God of the forefathers and the covenant, who fashioned man out of the dust and saved Israel from bondage, calling her to be His child. It is the God who summons man, through historic Israel, to the unique and solemn dignity of experiencing the ardour of His love, the fire of His wrath, the zeal of His jealousy and the final redeeming graciousness of His unchanging purpose.

Chapter Five

THE idea of revelation implied by the characteristics of the Hebrew prophetic consciousness raises in its most acute form the metaphysical problem of the relation between time and eternity. Prophetic revelation, we have insisted, does not consist in the supernatural disclosure of timeless abstract truth. It is rather the prophets' insight into the manifestation of the divine within the field of the temporal and the contingent. It is inextricably associated with the relativities of some particular time-situation. So far from being a didactic exposition of eternal truth concerning the nature of God, it has to do with the inspired announcement and interpretation of imminent events. Thus, Amos announces the coming rapid disintegration and overthrow of the northern kingdom as a social and political unit; Hosea foresees the divine vengeance upon the house of Jehu; Isaiah, the irresistible march of the Assyrian; Jeremiah, the irrevocably decreed destruction of Jerusalem. Revelation springs from the meeting of event with its adequate and rightful appreciation on the part of the prophet. It is the apprehension of certain temporal occurrences as peculiarly revelatory of that which transcends time. Such revelatory events constitute an irruption of eternity into time, and compose a meaningful sacred history—*Heilsgeschichte*—which unfolds itself at the heart of the time-series and lends divine purpose and significance to the whole.

Owing to this close blending of the temporal and eternal in the prophetic consciousness, it becomes almost impossible to detach the truth to which the prophets gave utterance from the historical setting which called it forth and to which it was immediately relevant. The prophetic word bears indelibly upon it the stamp of life as lived: it is struck out in the heat of some situation of direct urgency and need. This is in accordance with the fundamental bent of the Hebrew mind, with its aversion

from timeless metaphysic, its incapacity to grasp and
formulate abstract truth. The truth which the prophets
reveal is not in the first instance the truth of abstract
immutable principles (though these are deducible from
it), but a Word of God directed to the interpretation of
the momentous issues involved in some crucial moment
of time, or to the solution of some pressing problem that
has arisen out of the actual experience of living. It is an
illumination of the eternal aspect of some time-situation,
of the unplumbed depths of ontological reality that lie
behind the acts and decisions of men in time. From first
to last the prophets are concerned, not with the communication of an ethical or dogmatic system, nor even
with the precise forecast of future events, but with the
eternal Word of God addressed to the elect nation in
each successive, temporal phase of its corporate experience. The Word of God is itself timeless: but it strikes
home to men, in graciousness and mercy, or in judgment
and doom, precisely in and through the successiveness of
temporal experience. The Will of God is eternally valid:
it is essentially that which is, and therefore wholly
transcends time. But men's response to it, and their
growth in conformity with it, are tested and developed
by the measure in which they achieve its realization on
the temporal plane of history. This dynamic conception
of revelation raises, therefore, in its acutest form the
problem of the relation of eternity to time. For the
prophetic consciousness, each present moment points
beyond itself and is pregnant with divine meaning, and it
is in virtue of the depth and sincerity with which they
pierced to the inner spiritual significance of their times
that the prophets were able to convey a message of
abiding worth. They were intensely "men of the hour",
immersed in the *Sturm und Drang* of contemporary life.
Negatively, their most striking feature is just their utter
indifference to the systematic formulation of an abstract
truth which shall be valid for all time. The truth which
they uttered in their oracles was deeply coloured by the
particular circumstances to which it was immediately

relevant, and in the midst of which it arose. It was conditioned by and sharply orientated to the living needs
characteristic of a concrete historical situation: it was
heavily laden with *Aktualität*.

For the prophets, unlike the mystics, were not world-
renouncing: they did not seek refuge from the storms
of life in some inviolable haven of quietistic contemplation, and mystical absorption in the divine. They
lived, fought, struggled along with their contemporaries and compatriots: they experienced to the
full the heat and burden of the conflict into which
their energetic participation in the life of their times
plunged them. One of the main reasons for supposing
that Ezekiel's prophecies, prior to the fall of Jerusalem,
were originally uttered in the holy city itself, is that, like
all the original, spontaneous oracles of the prophets,
they bear stamped so visibly upon them the marks of
the great political and religious struggle whence they
emerged. They are born out of the fierce tumult, the
fluctuations and vicissitudes of a particular time-
situation, with its characteristic feeling-tone, its characteristic questionings, its characteristic fears: and in its
religious, psychological and political realities, their
raison d'être is to be sought. The same is true of all genuine
Hebrew prophecy, and the reason for this strong world-
affirming element, this naïve and whole-hearted absorption in the actualities of the hour, is just the prophets'
vivid sense of the reality of time, and of the vital urgency
of the issues bound up with each successive phase of the
national destiny. Each crisis of national life as it arises
is fraught with redemptive significance: it is a stage in
the unfolding *Heilsgeschichte*. Presenting the nation with
the inescapable necessity of decision, it offers the
opportunity of doing or of turning away from the Will
of God. In this inescapable demand which the temporal
phase of events makes upon the soul of man, the prophets
discern the impact of the Eternal upon the time-series,
confronting man in judgment yet waiting to break forth
in gracious redemptive love and mercy. Hence, we may

say that the prophets apprehend eternal truth and good through successive temporal situations in which that truth and good require to be embodied. Time is felt to be of supreme importance, and in its own degree to be utterly real, because in the conditions of human life it is the necessary medium through which man gains fellowship with the Eternal. The true path to this goal is not that of detachment from the successiveness of temporal existence (as though this successiveness were an insurmountable obstacle to spirituality) but of the right moral reaction to the situations which the changes and chances of time occasion.

Here, again, we note a striking contrast to the form of experience proper to mystical religion. The mystic, turning aside in world-weariness from the pain and disharmony of life and what is felt to be the confused welter of events in time, strips off one by one all the typical forms of human and sensuous experience and aspires to soar beyond the limitations incidental to temporality, until he reaches a state of timeless absorption in the Infinite. Rapt in this ecstatic consciousness, he feels that he is at last released from the bondage of time and sense and finitude. He is united to the everlasting Now. For the prophet, on the contrary, time is not a limitation to be transcended, but a sacramental reality. It does not stand over against Eternity in a relation of polarity as the Many is the antithesis of the One. In that sacred history wherein God is apprehended as self-revealing in redemptive action, time is indissolubly linked to Eternity in a relation far more vital and intimate than is the relation of substance to form, or body to clothes.

One of the best analogies to this fusion of time and Eternity in the prophetic awareness of *Heilsgeschichte* is furnished by the connexion of universal truth with local colour in great literature. In order to reveal and portray the permanent and universal characteristics of human nature, it is not necessary—indeed, it would be ruinous—that an author should attempt to divest his creations of the trappings which they derive from con-

temporary life. In the French classical tragedy of the
seventeenth century, the dramatist, with his cultured
concern for the universal and the abstract and his horror
of its concrete historical embodiment, made a systematic
attempt to remove his delineations from all the limiting
conditions special to the time and place of their origin.
He clothed them in the venerable garb of classical
antiquity in order to ensure the permanence and universality of their appeal. But when the French classical
tragedy becomes alive and grows to enduring greatness
in the hands of Racine, the inherent falseness of this
method becomes obvious: for it is easy to detect, in the
tragedies of Racine, the colourful and picturesque reality
of the *grand siècle* behind the thin classical disguise, and
the universality of their truth is not impaired by, but
springs from, the fidelity and depth with which he has
depicted human nature as he knew it in the everyday
life of his time. It is not by endeavouring to set aside all
that is local and particular in contemporary life, or by
deliberately striving to disentangle the eternal from the
temporal, the abstract from the concrete, that an artist
can most fruitfully hope to penetrate the secret of the
universal and permanent element in the complex web
of becoming. But it is by keeping his eye on the object,
it is in proportion to the piercing depth of his insight
into the very being of the concrete historical thing itself
and his capacity for reproducing it in its living concreteness and particularity, that an artist attains success in
creating works of art distinguished by the universality of
their truth and their abiding worth.

The inference from these observations is that the
universal and the timeless truths of physics and meta-
physics are intellectual abstractions from the real
world of becoming, and in man's experience are always
involved in their local and temporal embodiments.
It is impossible to manufacture the real out of such
abstractions, for, however complete our analysis may
be, living reality contains at its heart an element of
the mysterious and the given—an intractable surd

which is irreducible to abstract formulæ and defies all attempts at rationalization. It is with this element of the given—reality as experienced—that religion and art, as opposed to philosophy and science, have to do. Now, just as in art we find an indissoluble union of the universal and the particular, the permanent and the temporal, so, in the prophetic religious consciousness, it is not possible to dissociate the eternal—at least so far as the actuality of experience is concerned—from the time-series in which it is found to be inextricably involved. This inference raises the problem of the status of time and compels the conclusion that time is not some abstract geometrical framework within which the real (supposedly independent of time) is inserted, but that in some way time belongs to the very stuff of reality itself; in other words, time is in God.

Some philosophical schools posit an absolute antithesis between time and eternity. Time is a closed series with which it is not possible that eternity should come into direct relation. Likewise, nothing that happens in time can affect eternity itself. This, in the main, is the Greek conception of the relation existing between time and eternity. The Greek begins with a precise metaphysical definition of the two categories, and concludes that they are essentially incompatible and opposed to each other. Eternity is the realm of the perfect and the stable: time is the sphere of the imperfect, the ever-changing, the relatively unreal. There cannot be any vital connexion between the two: such relation as exists between them is statically, not dynamically, conceived. Time is a medium which distorts Eternity, as light is broken up in the colours of the prism. Again, since Eternity is defined as the perfect and the absolute, it follows logically that no actualization of the ideal in time can bring any positive enrichment to it. Time is a self-enclosed process, discontinuous with eternal life, of which it is but a pale, dim, reflection.[1] This Greek view of the matter has often

[1] This, in any event, is a predominant tendency in Greek thought, and receives clearest expression in Aristotle's view of the Eternal as the changeless who cannot enter into direct relation with the world

dominated classical Christian thought, and it is well expressed in the lines of Vaughan:

> *I saw Eternity the other night*
> *Like a great Ring of pure and endless light*
> *All calm as it was bright:—*
> *And round beneath it, Time in hours, days, years,*
> *Driven by the spheres*
> *Like a vast shadow moved. . . .*

When we turn to the Hebrew world-view, we find this whole cycle of assumptions contradicted. By the inherent limitations and characteristics of his mentality, the Hebrew is incapable of reaching any exact notion of what is involved in the concepts of time and eternity. He has to build wholly upon the practical nature of his experience in time. For the Hebrew, with his this-worldly emphasis, and lack of metaphysical insight, time was all. As the necessary framework of life, it filled his mental horizon. The idea of Eternity as the metaphysical opposite of time would have been to him an utterly unintelligible conception. He thinks of eternity as perpetual duration by contrast with mortal transience. The eternal life of God is a life indefinitely prolonged through vast reaches of time—not a life in which time is not. The Psalmist, contrasting the perishableness of his fleshly frame with the everlastingness of God, can find no other means of expressing the latter idea than that of saying that God's life spans all the great time-periods of human history. He naïvely applies to it the unit of years, thus suggesting that it is in principle of measurable duration.

> *Thy years are throughout all generations*
> *Thy years shall have no end. . . .*
>
> (Ps. 102: 24, 27.)

If God was to mean anything to the Hebrew, that meaning must be embodied in historic act and external circumstance. The actualities of earthly life had final significance for him. Every problem must find its solution within the arena of this terrestrial life. His ideal was expressed in the word *shalom*, which, like the Italian *virtu*—the ideal of Renaissance manhood—connoted the harmonious and integrated self-expression of the whole man. Heaven must be compressed into earth's tiny span: like Blake, the Hebrew saw "Eternity in an hour".

Yet, to state the matter thus without further qualification might be to invite serious misunderstanding. The Hebrew was no hedonist, even though the experiences of earthly life were, for him, endowed with supreme and utter reality. For the hedonist, time is important, because he is necessarily immersed in it and enclosed by it. It is the medium from which he must eagerly snatch a self-centred satisfaction. Yet, just becaue he is unable to transcend it, it sounds the death knell to all his bliss. The present, to which he feverishly clings, is but a vanishing point which is being perpetually engulfed in the insatiable past, and yielding to the swift onrush of the uncertain future. To live in time, in this purely super-ficial sense, is to be enchained by the fetters of an unreal and ever-dying existence. Despite the Hebrew's passion-ate attachment to the temporal mode of life, time must mean to him something more than this. For time, regarded in itself, is man's sovereign enemy, involving him in ever-increasing loss and ceaselessly negating all his gain. It is the very symbol of sin and death, express-ing all our misery, defeat and despair. Hence, we are faced by the paradox that, for the Hebrew, time was all; yet, in contrast to the hedonist position, time possessed for him a supreme spiritual significance and incarnated spiritual triumph. The creative vitality of his religion was such as to enable him to overcome the frustrations in-herent in time, even while apparently it afforded him no prospect of entering into a kingdom of eternal life which might lie beyond the bourne of time.

What is the meaning of this logical antinomy? We may express it quite simply, as follows. Time, religi-ously experienced by the Hebrew, implies Eternity as its necessary correlative, its sustaining background.

The Hebrew has no conception of Eternity and no dogmatic belief in eternal life, yet faith in the eternal and transcendent emerges as a logical implicate from his attitude towards time. The crux of the matter is clearly seen if we ask ourselves why time was felt by the Hebrew to possess ultimate importance. Time is important, for the hedonist, because it is a medium through which he is able to satisfy a personal need. Time is important, for the Hebrew, because it is the vehicle of an eternal demand; because it is the sphere in which man is confronted by the living God and experiences the pressure of divine Spirit. Upon man's response to that pressure depends the achievement of an eternal good, without which heaven would be forever impoverished. The spiritual fulfilment wrought by such lives as those of Job and Jeremiah is felt to be a veritable enrichment of eternity. Hence, the passionate emphasis which the Hebrew placed upon the actuality of the time-series was engendered by a religion which enabled him to transcend the negative aspect of the time-series. It was precisely through the realization of the spiritual possibilities inherent in time that the Hebrew gained his victory over the deathly element of time.

There thus emerges, from the Hebrew religious attitude towards time, a world-view which postulates the most vital and dramatic interrelation between time and eternity. Time is not a closed circle, cut adrift from ultimate being; but, on the contrary, eternity flows into time and gives it meaning. This world-view is the fundamental presupposition of the prophetic consciousness. The prophets are constituted prophets in virtue of their keen sense of the eternal impinging upon time through the concrete exigencies of some historical situation. Eternity is conceived, not formally and exoterically as static perfection, but spiritually, esoterically and dramatically. It is the creative movement of divine life, into which man's world is gathered up, and in the depths of which it is motivated. Every moment of time is "eschatological", bearing stamped upon it the divine demand,

and exposing the human response to that demand. Time is of ultimate importance because it is expressive of and contributory to eternity. The question whether the Will of God is done or not done in the actualities of history is of abiding and infinite import, because God Himself is not indifferent to it. Events in time matter to the Eternal, because time is somehow implicated in the inmost life of Eternity. It is contained within the eternal life of God. The realization of good in actual human living becomes a category of ultimate reality. Its existential quality, which is felt to hold the secret of the real, baffles a merely intellectual analysis and is not amenable to the formalist concepts of time and eternity. Although the Hebrew did not realize this, such an ultimate quality of living reality can only be adequately represented by the creative imagination of the artist.

The implicates of the prophetic consciousness thus lend revolutionary significance to the ancient problem of time and eternity. In opposition to the rationalist conception of eternity as a *Nunc Stans*, in which the time-process already exists as a completed whole, the prophetic consciousness implies the dynamic and spiritual notion of eternity as the purposive activity of God breaking in upon the time-process, informing it and redeeming it from insignificance. This is made particularly clear by Deutero-Isaiah in whose work we see that Yahwe is able to foretell the future course of events, not for the metaphysical reason that temporal distinctions are not valid for the divine mind, but because the future is conceived as something which flows from the creative divine will and is shaped through the divine control of human volitions. Time is real because it is the sphere in which God works. The purpose and counsel of Yahwe stand: they confer upon history such reality as it possesses. For the Hebrew prophet, no logical problem is involved in these conceptions, which in their quasi-mythological freshness are repugnant to the spirit of philosophy and science. He is not haunted by the notion—common to Plato and Newton and strenuously opposed by Bergson

—that time is a uniform system of measurement which exists independently of its concrete filling. Nor does he conceive eternity as the simultaneity of the perfect changeless One, in which the multiple successiveness of the temporal order vanishes. He accepts the world of individualized, historical experience, the world of the irreducibly given, without endeavouring to square it with some kinematical scheme. This, for him, is the Real; and its reality is rooted in the activity of God, who is ceaselessly impinging upon the soul of man.

Chapter Six

HISTORY

THAT interpretation of time and eternity which the prophetic consciousness implies is one which gives birth to the idea of history. History springs from the dramatic interaction of time and eternity. It is the self-revealing and redeeming activity of God in time which renders the process of events a true and significant succession, interpretable in terms of purpose and mind. Without this element of spiritual meaning, history cannot be said to exist at all; it degenerates into a chaos of mere reversible happenings. An event, as distinguished from a factual occurrence, is something that possesses significance for mind: it is constituted by the irreducible synthesis of happening and its apprehension. The Hebrew prophets are the first philosophers of history because they apprehend events as a significant whole, determined and fashioned by the eternal creative principle, which, while transcending them, is ever active within them.

In this respect the Hebrew prophets are decisively differentiated from the scientific historian and psychologist who, interpreting events solely from the standpoint of humanistic scholarship, will seek to explain them in terms of efficient causation. But their ultimate revealing quality will have escaped his analysis, because he will have viewed them solely with reference to their determination by this-worldly conditions, material and economic, and by the fascinating play of motive in the human soul. But the prophet is not a historian in this sense. His standpoint is essentially different. He is concerned uniquely to bring out this ultimate revealing significance which emanates from the fact that God is the unseen, all-controlling protagonist in the drama of human history. The prophet is indifferent to the immediate causation of events discoverable by the investigation of the intellect alone; it is his aim to illuminate their ultimate causation which lies in the steadfast purpose and counsel of Yahwe. The distinction between the historian and the prophet can perhaps best be illustrated by an analogy drawn from the sphere of mathematical dimensions. If we could imagine a creature living in a two-dimensional world and then consider the contrast which would obtain between the truths relative to his surface geometry and those relative to our three-dimensional cosmos, we shall have some dim adumbration of the contrast which lies between the scientific and the prophetic understanding of history. The scientific historian moves on a two-dimensional plane. His conclusions, verified by exact research, are true, but true only within the limits and the relativities of the world-view which conditions his interpretation. The prophet sees events taking shape within a new perspective, that not of time only, but of eternity. He introduces the dimension opened up by the eternal creative activity of God, impinging upon time from the transcendental world and constituting the very essence and truth, furnishing the fundamental possibility, of all events whatsoever. Thus the prophet glimpses, and with overmastering conviction, announces, the ontological Reality which is self-expressive through historical events. In other words, he sees history as God's continous act of creation. This is what is meant when we speak of the prophet as divining the revelatory significance which shines through the historical process. For the prophet, history flows from the eternal purpose of God for man, and signifies the actual realization of that purpose.

This conception of history as the workmanship of God is inwrought in the very essence of the prophetic consciousness. The mission of the prophets of Israel consisted largely in orientating the spiritual destiny of the nation by reading and inculcating the right divine meaning which controlled the events of their time. The consciousness which gave birth to their sense of vocation was that of being in possession of the secret divine purpose which overshadowed the confused interplay of contemporary and forthcoming events. They were the exponents of the inner spiritual history of Israel which lay concealed beneath the husk of Israel's outward fortunes. They were able to do this because they saw the history of their times as the earthly reflection of a heavenly drama. For them it was the story of a dramatic, relentless, conflict between man and God. Their interpretation of history is parallel to their interpretation of man. Just as they realize that the true explanatory principle of man's nature is to be sought in his inescapable relatedness to God, so history for them is no predetermined system, no self-evolving idea, but the scene of a continuous interaction between the spirit of man and the spirit of God. It is the sphere of "realized eschatology". Each successive phase of the process is pregnant with the eschatological significance which will be outwardly and vividly embodied in the Day of the Lord. Thus, Amos saw that the current eschatology was dead and false because it was glaringly contradicted by the vital spiritual eschatology implicit in the context of daily events. Thus, the prophets fathomed the mystery of the dynamic relation between man and God which the outward shape of events concealed. Whereas the historian would interpret Israel's apostasy as the natural wisdom of a people which felt an obligation to propitiate the gods of the conquered territory, or as the corruptions inevitably attendant upon advancing civilization, the prophets are haunted by the eternal divine meaning of this apostasy. They hear the passionate plaints and pleadings of Yahwe, who finds His gracious love and fidelity despised; by using the symbol of marriage and adultery, they suggest the deep personal nature of the tragedy. Yahwe pleads the monstrous unnaturalness of the crime: "Can a maid forget her ornaments or a bride her attire? Yet My people have forgotten Me days without number" (Jer. 2: 32).

Further, the far-ranging vision of the prophets imposes

spiritual unity upon the world's history as a whole. All
its complex, multifarious, movements are brought under
the secure control of the divine purpose; and the judging,
redeeming, activity of God is detected as manifesting
itself within them. This, however, does not mean simply
that the actions of good men in time are intrinsically
revealing of the divine. The prophets imply that Yahwe
is sovereign Lord of the entire process of events in which
good and evil mingle confusedly. Yahwe is apprehended
as being decisively active even in those events which
appear most flagrantly to deny Him. The prophets
apprehend the interaction of the divine and human, not
as an immanentist unfolding of divine significance at the
heart of human life, but rather as a clash of wills in which
the divine Spirit is revealed with a piercing and inescapable challenge. There is, as it were, a vertical descent
of the divine Word upon the horizontal time-stream,
illuminating in judgment the ultimate significance of
men's actions and in mercy rendering them instrumental
to its own redemptive purpose for humanity. It is in this
way that history becomes revelatory of God. On a
superficial view, history appears as a chain of efficient
causation—a complex of events, good and bad, motivated in the interplay of human wills. If history could be
thus written off as being simply the outcome of human
motives, it could never be said to reveal God. It becomes
revelatory of God when it is seen as a process which is
rooted in eternity and takes its rise from the divine
initiative. It gathers its abiding heavenly significance
from the fact that man on the historical plane is sharply
confronted by God. It is a living synthesis wherein the
divine is manifested even in the face of actions which
are a defiant negation of it. This is possible because in
the vision of the prophets all events whatsoever are
envisaged as being subjected to the overruling omnipotence of God and as rendered subservient to the ends
which He has chosen. The actions of the king of Assyria,
viewed from the angle of man and his space-time world,
may be characterized as determined by lust and ambi-

tion, and, with striking realism and sense of character, the prophet puts before us the overweening thoughts which surge up in the conqueror's heart (Isa. 10: 7–11). But the characteristic note of the passage—that which stamps it as springing from the inspired insight of the prophet, rather than from the mood of the artist or the historian—is that this piece of psychological analysis is given a supernatural setting and pictured in strictest relation to the thought of God. Just when the will of the human agent, in its pride and egoism, is seen in sharpest conflict with all that we mean by the divine, and would therefore seem to be most stubbornly self-determined in rebellion against God, it is represented as the instrument for the fulfilment of a divine purpose. The savage conquests of the Assyrian, though proceeding from brutal lust, are yet the means by which Yahwe makes manifest to Israel the divine condemnation of its sin. Still more striking is the prophetic interpretation of the Exile—an event which seemed to give the lie to the covenants and promises, and which, according to the nationalistic theology of the times, indicated the defeat of Yahwe at the hands of a foreign power. Jeremiah put forward the revolutionary view that Yahwe, so far from suffering frustration through the Exile, was Himself the determining cause of it. Nebuchadnezzar is described as Yahwe's servant (Jer. 25: 9). To the prophet, it seemed that the volitional activity of God was so palpably manifest in the Babylonian conquest that to resist the Babylonian armies as they stormed the gates of Jerusalem was equivalent to resisting the will of God Himself (Jer. 21: 5). Yahwe, in His inscrutable counsels, effects tragic calamity, and originates destructive commotions in which nations are hurled against each other: He stands the silent unseen Actor in scenes "where ignorant armies clash by might". Amos exclaims: "Shall evil befall a city and the Lord hath not done it?" (3: 6). Jeremiah is bidden take the cup of the Lord's fury and cause all the nations to drink it, thus making woe and desolation descend upon them (25: 15 ff.). Yahwe hands over Egypt to the King of

Babylon as a reward for the service rendered by the latter in punishing Tyre (Ezek. 29: 18, 19).

This faith in the all-controlling and triumphant purpose of Yahwe reaches its most sublime and ample expression in the prophecies of Deutero-Isaiah. No other prophet pictures so vividly the intensity and energy of Yahwe's volitional activity as manifested in the events of history. The complex ramifications of world-politics are fashioned and governed by Yahwe for the purpose of exhibiting His wrath and mercy towards Israel (Isa. 42: 23 ff.; 43: 1 ff.). The Return, which a critical historian would estimate simply as a by-product of a certain phase of world-history, becomes charged with a momentous spiritual significance because it is viewed as the saving activity of God mediated through human agents who appear to be working out their own will. Cyrus, the heathen conqueror, is spoken of in mystical terms which exalt him to the position of an elect, anointed servant of God, specially consecrated to be the instrument with which the Lord brings His redemption nigh (Isa. 44: 24 ff.; 45: 1 ff.).

Thus, for the prophets, there was no possibility of distinguishing between secular and sacred history. All was *Heilsgeschichte*—the manifestation of God's purpose in judgment and redemption. All events that affected the life of the Israelite were woven into the warp and woof of the nation's dramatic relationship with God. Such a view of history presupposes that intimate mingling of time and eternity which we have seen to be so vital an implication of the prophetic consciousness. The spiritual and interior divine life becomes exteriorized in historic event, representing an irruption of Eternity into Time— a process in which the temporal and contingent by becoming united with the eternal divine Will is redeemed from the inherent corruption which vitiates it. The prophets show us the victory of God being wrought out at the heart of time.

Yahwe's Lordship of history is exercised through His control of human volitions. This does not mean that the actors in the drama are robbed of their free initiative, or are forcibly prevented from working out their own evil will. It is impossible to eliminate from the process the element of the contingent which springs from the unruly wills and affections of sinful men. But if we could gain, with the prophet, a synoptic view of the process as a whole, the whole would be seen as grounded in and ultimately determined by the Will of God and as held securely in the grasp of divine omnipotence. However sharply the rebellious and self-assertive will of man may run counter to the Will of God, the supreme sway of the latter is not in the least diminished, but rather expresses its supremacy afresh in its characteristic reaction to, and control of, the new situation which man's free choice has brought into being. An event which is immediately caused by the evil will of man is seen to fall within the dimension of Eternity, and to witness, negatively, by opposition, to the victorious reality of Spirit which it seems most emphatically to deny. The evil will is thus self-frustrating and self-stultifying; just when it accomplishes most defiantly its egoistic ends, it is made to subserve and promote the divine will which overrules and controls it. The records of Israel's history have been moulded by the prophets and their schools under the dominance of this conviction. Thus, Joseph can say of an event to the production of which the evil passions of man have notably contributed: "So now it was not you that sent me hither, but God" (Gen. 45: 8). It is a philosophy of history which receives its crowning illustration from the inexhaustible spiritual significance of the Crucifixion of Jesus—the supreme explosive encounter of man and God on the plane of the historical process.

This view of history is thus one which leads to the formulation of the doctrine of Divine Providence. We have seen that the prophets envisage history as a process in which time and eternity may achieve the completest spiritual union. They illuminate the fact that the result transcends man's intention, and is never completely predictable from the antecedent elements which go to its making. This is so, because the achieved synthesis, flowing from the dramatic clash of divine and human wills, represents the emergence into reality of something rich, novel, vital, not exhaustively explainable in terms of its tangible causes. It is an effect which cannot even be rightly analysed into its divine and human elements. In its mysterious richness and fullness it evades all analysis, as it defies all prediction that is based merely upon human calculation and the human attempt to imagine possible re-combinations of its constituent antecedents. Thus the future can never be predicted simply by the re-shuffling of elements contained in the present because it is something which in its newness expands the being of the present. This truth is clearly brought to light by the prophet Isaiah, who characteristically rebukes the folly of those who would place their trust in political sagacity and foresight (20: 5, 6; 29: 14, 15; 30: 1–ff.; 31: 1–ff.). Political wisdom, however astute, cannot foretell the future, for the simple reason that the future is the creative work of God—a unity in duality which is not calculable from the plans of the human actors in what is essentially a divine-human drama. Hence the striking originality of his definition of religion. The religious spirit requires the renunciation of human striving and of confident human planning, for the wisdom of the wise is confounded and frustrated by the creative activity of God. The machinations of political life cannot be made contributory to the fulfilment of a divine end. Religion requires an exclusive trust in Yahwe, a quiet and confident waiting for the emergence of His work upon the plane of human history. The seeing eye of the religious man pierces the vortex of contemporary political strife and beholds the sure establishment of Yahwe's work. It is the busy and the worldly-wise "who regard not the work of the Lord, neither have they considered the operation of His hands" (Isa. 5: 12). These original affirmations of Isaiah illuminate as in a lightning flash the inner spiritual creativity and dynamism of history. History evinces at its heart the creative life of

Eternal Spirit, ever transcending the physical, biological and psychological determinations of events.

It is because the prophet is endowed with penetrating insight into the interior spiritual dynamic of history that he is able to foretell, and that the capacity to foretell may with justice be regarded as his most distinctive gift. To the scientific historian who operates only in the relativities of space-time, history is static and is dominated by time. Such a one is locked in the vanishing point of the present. The present, for him, is cut off equally from the "no more" and the "not yet". Past and future are lifeless nonentities. The one needs to be laboriously resuscitated by the methods of exact scholarship; the other lies entombed in the dark unknown, utterly inaccessible to human gaze. But the prophet is constituted a prophet just because he transcends the relativity of this human standpoint, and is able to view history *sub specie alternitatis*. He looks down upon it from a vantage-point which is utterly incommensurable with the scientific standpoint. He sees time as expressive of eternity. Past, present and future, are for him vitally interlinked in one unbroken dynamic sequence. He stands, as it were, outside time. The tragic drama of history is interiorized, in the prophetic vision, as an integral element of eternity. It becomes a transcendent, living, unity in which past, present and future are fused. History is a continuous movement in which the creative life of Spirit is being realized, and therefore he who is in constant touch with the primal Source of all being is able to comprehend in one all-embracing vision the spiritual movement and fufilment which impart to history its meaning. It cannot be too emphatically asserted that, for the prophetic consciousness, history is essentially dynamic and dramatic. It is a movement pregnant with significance because it originates in the tragic clash of divine and human wills: it is the tragic conflict of man with God becoming resolved into a triumphant spiritual unity. Hence the characteristic rhythm of prophecies of woe and prophecies of restoration, prophecies of exile and prophecies of return. Hence the supreme importance of eschatology, of Messianic fulfilment for the Hebrew religious consciousness. Hence, too, we realize the significance of the definition that the prophet is one who *foretells*. He foretells because he is able to transcend time, because he realizes that history is a drama which primarily and fundamentally takes place in eternity, just as history gathers its ever-living meaning from the fact that, in it, the life of eternity is projected into time. Behind the stubborn clinging to the idea that the prophet is one who is able to *foretell*, we detect the profound and ancient wisdom of the East.

Finally, the prophetic attitude to history is conclusive for the characterization of prophetic-Biblical religion, in sharp contradistinction to religions of the mystical-ecstatic type. It is well known that the latter are indifferent to history, and, indeed, contradict the very conception of history as a meaningful and revelatory process. For the true mystic, history is swallowed up in eternity: it is a flux of "multitudinous particular phenomena", apparent rather than real, from which he seeks emancipation by philosophic wisdom and the cultivation of an interior spirituality. For the prophet, on the other hand, the historical event is the focus of revelation, a sacramental expression of the divine Word, judging and redeeming man; man in history is brought under the sovereignty of a God who speaks, who takes the initiative in the redemption of the human soul, and whose divine Providence, in the shaping of circumstance, confronts man with the necessity for making a historic and spiritually significant decision. God is continuously operative within history as Redeemer and Judge; history partly reveals and partly hides Him. *It is not an indefinitely extended process, not a cyclical process, but a dynamic, cumulative, revealing process, developing towards some transcendent goal—in short, a process which forms the proper sphere for Messianic expectations.*

Conclusion

TOWARDS A HEBREW-CHRISTIAN METAPHYSIC

THOSE philosophical repercussions of the Hebrew prophetic consciousness which have been the subject of our argument have consequences of the utmost importance for Christian theology. Indeed, they lead us towards the formulation of a world-view which furnishes a sure metaphysical basis for the central affirmations of the Christian faith concerning the Incarnation and the Atonement. The special characteristics of this Hebraic-Christian metaphysic emerge in sharpest contrast to what we might term the Hellenic outlook. The essence of the Hellenic consciousness is the intellectual vision of the world of pure being, decisively separated from the world of becoming. The ultimate Reality is idealized in the form of logical concepts which are put forward·as an adequate representation of it. The essence of divinity is defined by means of clear and distinct ideas. Eternity is set over against Time as the perfect against the imperfect, the absolute against the relative, the unchanging against the transient: the unimaginable plenitude of the divine life is opposed to the ceaseless flux of human affairs which are without ultimate significance and goal. The utmost that man can do in his small world of becoming, and upon his lower plane of reality, is to strive to achieve an imitation of that eternal perfection of which he catches a glimpse in moments of contemplation. But his achievements, however splendid, can have no final value, since there is no possibility of a real and vital interpenetration of the two worlds.

In contrast with this static system of ideas, we find ourselves confronted, in Hebrew prophetic literature, with a creative religion which is relative to Hebrew anthropology and which in its very vitality resists formulation in intellectual terms. Here, the point of departure is the polar opposite to that which leads to the special consciousness of the Greeks. The presupposition of this peculiar prophetic awareness of the divine is not the validity of logical concepts, but the validity of man's total life-experience, and the ever-present possibility of a numinous confrontation by God on the plane of historical reality. The essential factor in this type of consciousness is the intuition, strengthened and verified in practical experience, of the utter and final significance of the time-series—the sphere in which God becomes redemptively known to man. The real, so far from being formalized and petrified in static concepts, is experienced in the dramatic clashes and crises of actual living, is encountered in the sweeping dynamic rhythms of history which is ever developing to some meaningful end. There is no philosophical notion of eternity, only a sure personal grasp of the eternal life, the transcendent holiness, the moral steadfastness of God, guaranteeing the ever-renewed salvation of man. "For I am the Lord, I change not; therefore are ye sons of Jacob not consumed" (Mal. 3: 6). Just as there is no *a priori* philosophy of the soul as an immortal entity, but only the swift poetic intuition that God's eternal life ensures the durability of man's communion with Him, so there is no metaphysical definition of the essence of divinity and eternity, but, instead, the indissoluble certainty of God as the transcendent Worker whose creative and redemptive activity gathers all history into a unity of permanent significance and endows it with the victorious quality of eternity.

In a metaphysical scheme appropriate to these prophetic intuitions we might say that time is the symbol of man's frailty and creatureliness. It expresses the fact that he is *basar*, in contrast with the divine *ruach*. It spells his perishability, his inescapable limitedness, his essential helplessness apart from God. It indicates his perpetual experience of loss and defeat, negation and frustation; it means his incapacity to hold and enjoy in his limited time-span more than an infinitesimal fraction of the infinite reality. No one has better expressed the poignancy of man's sinful experience of time than Baudelaire:

Souviens-toi que le Temps est un joueur avide
Qui gagne sans tricher, à tout coup! c'est la loi,
Le jour décroît; la nuit augmente, Souviens-toi!
Le gouffre a toujours soif; le clepsydre se vide.

This victory of mere, unredeemed Time, however, signifies ultimate death: in the Hebrew-Christian world-view, time is the outward form of man's life and is capable of being filled with a divine content which transforms its negative aspect and makes it a partaker of the quality of eternity. Time may be so inwrought with divine meaning as to become an integral element of the divine experience in eternity. Time and eternity are not logical concepts involving a logical antimony, but symbols expressive of spiritual states, time that is unredeemed expressing the helpless state of creaturely fallen man, eternity expressing the freedom and victory of creative spirit. The concrete historical objective form of events in time is but the condition of man's creaturely apprehension of their inner spiritual subjective substance which is rooted in eternity. The dynamic spiritual subjective attitude towards time and eternity, as opposed to the static objective metaphysical formalization of them, makes possible a fusion of the two spheres in the depths of personal spirit. Such is the metaphysic implied in the powerful prophetic sense of Israel's history as a *Heilsgeschichte*, as a drama wrought out in God's eternity. The very conception of history as a meaningful whole is in fact impossible unless the time-process is in some way ultimately real. For history means that the chain of events in time is a converging dramatic process which has a real beginning and a real ending. It is constituted such a significant process by the impact of reality upon time, apprehended in moments of tension and crisis when sinful man stands confronted by redemptive, living God. The very essence of the prophetic consciousness is the piercing vision which apprehends the interaction of the two orders of being, and therefore appreciates the meaning of history. The dramatic clash of time and eternity means a struggle between life and death principles: it signifies the call of God's love to man and the character of man's response.

The implication of a passible element in the divine being is also vitally connected with the prophetic philosophy of history. If history is the sphere in which a divine-human drama is taking place that is invested with the quality of ultimate reality, then God must not be primarily regarded as the ineffable, the unknowable, the impassible; but, rather, as the God who speaks, whose prevenient activity conditions man's doing and thinking, and who reacts with all the intensity of personal Being to the spiritual significance of events in time. God as the self-existent eternal, absolute Being, is not cut off from the roots of history but is prior to and within history, and it is indeed only in virtue of this divine prevenience, this interpenetration with eternity, that history stands forth as a meaningful process. Too often, discussions of the passibility of God seem to presuppose that God is to be likened to a spectator standing outside the tumult of human history and experiencing or failing to experience emotions such as anger, sorrow, sympathy, pity, which toss within the human heart. Such a view is naïvely naturalistic, and entirely fails to reach down to the deep centre of the problem. When we say that the historical process has ultimate significance and that God is passible—thus drawing out and emphasizing the implications of the prophetic consciousness—we are using symbolical language to express one absolute truth which is irreducible to rational concepts, the truth, namely, that the transcendent is also the immanent, that the Spirit of the Lord fills the world, that the inner spiritual meaning of history—deriving from the impact of Logos upon the awakening human spirit—is gathered up as a moment in the eternal life of God. The prophetic ascription of an emotional consciousness to God is not to be taken literally, naïvely, and realistically, but rather to be regarded as a piece of mythological creation enshrouding a deeper truth concerning the mysteries of divinity and humanity than any which is expressible through the medium of man's rationalized surface consciousness. This truth is that man's life in its ethical and spiritual reaches is no mere epiphenomenon arising in the course of a meaningless process, but that, on the contrary, it has its roots in the deep zone of ultimate being. Thus, the dualism of God and man, of the divine and natural worlds—a dualism which a falsely rational orientation of thought tends to emphasize—is overcome in the inner depths of creative spirit and life. This does not mean that through the spiritual development of the human consciousness the distinction between the human and the divine tends to be obliterated (for such a view would involve us in the pantheism which ever attends an exaggerated mysticism) but rather that God, while remaining in His inexhaustible mystery and infinitude essentially distinct from man, yet is unimaginably near to man as the immanent Principle inspiring man's spiritual life and determining the spiritual aspect of man's actions.

GENERAL INDEX

INDEX

Nomadic religion of Israel, 101

Numinous, fear of, 27; reactions to, 42; energy in holy man, 46; power, 103

OMEN, REVEALING, 44; observation of, 51; Amos' divination from, 55

One, the, all-embracing, 27; as the Absolute in mystical negative theology, 132

Oracle, priestly, 34; ephod, 39

PAIN, INSENSIBILITY TO, 24

Palestine, ecstatic phenomena of, 53, 85

Pantheism, 136

Pascal, 127

Passibility of God implied by prophetic consciousness, 138, 141, Concl., 175

Pathos, divine, prophet's sympathy with, 138 ff.; expresses numinous conception of deity, 144 f.; co-relative of God's personal holiness, 144 f.; makes possible manifold forms of relation between man and God, 145; personal reaction of God to sin, 145; Hosea's vision of, 146; not incompatible with divine joy and omnipotence, 147 f.

Paul, St., 92, 124

Pelatiah, death of, 49, 57

Personality, Hebrew conception of, 8; dissolution of, in ecstatic experience of union and absorption, 28, 132 f.; self-revealing personality of the prophet, 28, 124; in God, an essential implicate of the prophetic consciousness, 129 ff.; required by a satisfying philosophy of value, 130 ff.; felt as an obstacle by the mystical consciousness, 133; excluded by a rigorous definition of God as the Absolute, 133 f.; demanded by dramatic character of prophets' religious experience and its note of duality in unity, 134; idea of, considered as a principle of unification, 135 ff.; supplies key to an understanding of God's relation with the world, 136 f.; a symbolic concept only in relation to the Godhead, 137; division of, in Isaiah, 61 f.; diffused through bodily organs, 66 f.; involves divine pathos, 145

Persons, knowledge of, 114 f.

Plato, 160

Pratt, 97

Priest-prophets, 80 f.

Priest allied with *nabi*, 83

Prophet, true, penetrates hidden laws of reality, 54; canonical, refuses to admit current explanation of prophecy,

64; association with priest, 70 f.; true order of, 72; writing prophet belongs to *nabi* movement, 79; fine flower of *nabi* movement, 80; is differentiated from priest-prophet by necessity for making a venture of faith, 87 f.; false, 53, 71, 77 f., 84 ff., 86 ff. *See also Nabi.*

Prophetic consciousness, Hebrew, its differentation from the ecstatic type of religion, 26 ff.; inseparable from background of nation's corporate religious life, 31 f.; the characteristic sense of possession, 60 f.; interpreted by the Hebrew notion of the divine *ruach*, 62 ff.; reserve of the canonical prophet in accepting this interpretation, 64; relation of the *ruach* to the human personality of the prophet, 64 f.; divine control of physiological impressions, 66 f.; prophet realistically conceived as the mouthpiece of God, 68 f.; its authority intrinsic, 87 f.; part played by ecstasy, peripheral and accidental, 80 f., 94; a state of the highest integration and enhancement of being, 96 f.; characterized by passivity and vivid awareness of value, 96; mental mechanism underlying it psychologically analysed, 97 ff.; assurance of contact with Ultimate Reality expressed in the phrase *Ko amar Yahwe*, 99 f.; its final ground is the soul's confrontation by the living God and response in self-commitment and trust, 102 ff.; implies an existential theology, 111 f.; its authority may not be appropriately tested by the criterion of mere reason, 117 ff.; its validity properly recognizable only by an act of spiritual insight, 119 ff.; has to do with the relativities of a space-time situation, 151 ff.; raises metaphysical problem of time and eternity, 152; consists in prophet's grasp of secret divine purpose which controls events and gives rise to the sacred history of Israel, 164; implies insight into the interior spiritual dynamism of history and the capacity to foretell, 170 ff.

Providence, doctrine of, 168 f.

Psyche, spiritual, 29 f.; physical, 30

QOSEM (diviner), 23, 34, 37

RABBINIC DIALECTICS OF ST. PAUL, 124

Racine, 155

Rain charm, 47

Rainmaker, 45 ff.

INDEX OF SCRIPTURE REFERENCES